Preparing Students for
Standardized Testing

Grade 4

By
JANET P. SITTER, Ph.D.

COPYRIGHT © 2004 Mark Twain Media, Inc.

ISBN 1-58037-266-X

Printing No. CD-1626

Mark Twain Media, Inc., Publishers
Distributed by Carson-Dellosa Publishing Company, Inc.

Table of Contents

Table of Contents (cont.)

Introduction

Standardized tests are designed to measure how well a student has learned the basic knowledge and skills that are taught in elementary and middle schools. They generally cover the content areas of reading, vocabulary, language, spelling, math, science, and social studies. The most recent standardized tests also focus on the student's ability to think critically. It would be unrealistic, however, to expect that students will know (or have been taught) all of the material on the tests. Some of this material will be new to students, and this may cause anxiety in both students and teachers.

The purpose of this book is to help you familiarize your students with the format and language of tests, with important test-taking strategies, and with practice in the content areas of the major standardized tests used nationally. These include:

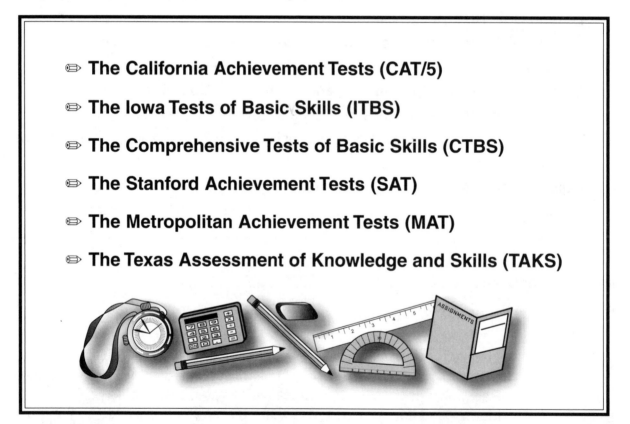

- **The California Achievement Tests (CAT/5)**

- **The Iowa Tests of Basic Skills (ITBS)**

- **The Comprehensive Tests of Basic Skills (CTBS)**

- **The Stanford Achievement Tests (SAT)**

- **The Metropolitan Achievement Tests (MAT)**

- **The Texas Assessment of Knowledge and Skills (TAKS)**

By spending 20 minutes a day for three weeks prior to the administration of the standardized test for your school district and grade level and using the material in this book, you will not only increase your students' confidence in their test-taking skills but also help them to successfully demonstrate their knowledge and skills. *Preparing Students for Standardized Testing* will provide your students with opportunities to take practice tests under similar conditions to those that exist on standardized tests. Teachers should photocopy the practice tests in the book and the practice answer sheets for students to use. This will familiarize students with the process of filling in computer-scored answer sheets. In order to better prepare your students for standardized testing, it may be beneficial to set a time limit you think is appropriate for the average student in your class.

Content Area Skills

Reading

Word Analysis:
- ✔ Identify prefixes, suffixes, root words
- ✔ Recognize figurative language
- ✔ Demonstrate knowledge of structural relationships in letters, words, signs

Vocabulary:
- ✔ Identify synonyms, antonyms, homophones, palindromes
- ✔ Recognize word origins and words in context
- ✔ Demonstrate knowledge of multiple meanings of words

Comprehension:
- ✔ Identify main idea and supporting details
- ✔ Recognize theme, story elements, and author's purpose
- ✔ Demonstrate literal/interpretive understanding
- ✔ Distinguish cause/effect, reality/fantasy
- ✔ Demonstrate critical understanding by drawing conclusions, making predictions, and extending meaning to other contexts

Language

Mechanics:
- ✔ Identify the appropriate use of capitalization, punctuation, and parts of speech in text
- ✔ Recognize correct spelling in text
- ✔ Identify misspelled words in text

Expression:
- ✔ Identify topic, concluding, and supporting sentences in text
- ✔ Determine correct usage, sequence of ideas, and relevance of information
- ✔ Recognize connective/transitional words, phrases, and sentences
- ✔ Identify and correct errors in existing text and in text written by the student

Information Skills:
- ✔ Identify parts of a book
- ✔ Recognize and use dictionary and other reference materials
- ✔ Demonstrate the ability to understand and interpret maps, charts, and diagrams

Content Area Skills (cont.)

Mathematics

Concepts:
- ✔ Identify, compare, and order numbers and number operations
- ✔ Recognize and compare equivalent numbers
- ✔ Interpret and apply numbers in real-world situations
- ✔ Demonstrate knowledge of estimation, place value, expanded notation, rounding, Roman numerals, time, geometric shapes, and planes, rays, angles, parallel, and perpendicular

Computation:
- ✔ Identify the properties and relationships of number and operations
- ✔ Recognize and extend patterns, transformations, symmetry, and geometric figures
- ✔ Recognize and solve real-world computation problems
- ✔ Demonstrate proficiency in computation procedures in addition, subtraction, multiplication, division, decimals, and fractions

Problem Solving and Reasoning:
- ✔ Identify and apply problem-solving strategies to real-world problems
- ✔ Recognize and interpret data in models, diagrams, pictures, and graphs
- ✔ Use a variety of estimation strategies; determine reasonableness of results
- ✔ Demonstrate inductive/deductive reasoning and spatial and proportional reasoning to solve real-world problems

Science

Process and Inquiry:
- ✔ Identify scientific principles, processes, and inquiry
- ✔ Interpret and make reasonable interpretations from scientific data
- ✔ Recognize use of inferences to draw conclusions
- ✔ Demonstrate an understanding of fundamental concepts of scientific inquiry

Concepts:
- ✔ Identify life cycles of plants and animals; understand the term *habitat*
- ✔ Understand the water cycle and the terms *decomposers*, *fossil fuel*, *eclipse*, *buoyancy*
- ✔ Understand societal issues such as recycling and pollution
- ✔ Recognize basic principles of earth (e.g., rocks, minerals, earthquakes, volcanoes) and space (e.g., air, planets, solar systems)
- ✔ Demonstrate knowledge of basic health and nutrition for the human body

Content Area Skills (cont.)

Social Studies

History and Cultures:
✔ Identify famous people, holidays, symbols, customs, norms, and social institutions in the United States and connect historical events to them
✔ Recognize the contributions, influences, and interactions of various cultures
✔ Recognize patterns of similarities in different historical times
✔ Use time lines, product and global maps, and cardinal directions
✔ Demonstrate an historical understanding of time, continuity, and societal change in the United States and the world

Civics and Government:
✔ Identify government bodies and characteristics of good citizenship
✔ Recognize the roles and responsibilities of government and citizens
✔ Demonstrate an understanding of the basic principles of government
✔ Understand the democratic process

Economics:
✔ Identify economic principles of supply/demand, consumer/producer, goods/services, profit/loss
✔ Recognize three roles individuals play: worker, consumer, citizen
✔ Demonstrate an understanding of how the general social/political/economic environment affects opportunity and happiness
✔ Understand economic concepts related to products, jobs, and the environment

Geography:
✔ Identify and use geographic terms to describe land forms, bodies of water, weather, and climate
✔ Recognize how human use of the environment is influenced by cultural values, economic wants, level of technology, and environmental perceptions
✔ Demonstrate geographic methods to interpret maps, graphs, charts, and photographs
✔ Understand global and environmental issues
✔ Locate continents, major countries, resources, and regions

The Language of Tests

Here are some of the most frequently used terms in assessment.

Accountability: The practice of evaluating teachers and schools based on measurable goals

Achievement Test: Tests designed to measure knowledge and skills, usually objective, standardized, and norm-referenced

Alternative Assessment: Methods of evaluating student work and progress that are *not* traditional standardized tests (e.g., portfolios, anecdotal records, teacher observation, interviews, performance, demonstration projects, etc.)

Assessment: A systematic method for testing student progress and achievement

Authentic Assessment: The tasks and procedures used for assessment are closely related to tasks found in the real world.

Content Validity: The extent to which the content of a test actually measures the knowledge and skills the test claims to measure

Criterion-referenced Test: A test that measures a student's performance to a predetermined measure of success, rather than to a norm group

Curricular Validity: The extent to which a test measures what has been taught

Diagnostic Test: A test used to assess specific characteristics in order to make instructional decisions

Evaluation: The process of making judgments and instructional decisions obtained from a form of assessment

Grade Equivalent Score: A measure that compares a student's raw score on a standardized test to average scores across grade levels

Group Test: A test that is administered to more than one student at the same time

Individual Test: A test that is administered to only one student at a time

Intelligence Test: A test that measures a student's general mental ability or scholastic aptitude

Mean: The average of a set of test scores

Median: The middle score of a set of test scores

Minimum-competency Test: A test that measures whether a student has attained the minimum level of overall achievement necessary for a particular purpose

The Language of Tests (cont.)

Mode: The most frequent score of a group of scores

National Standards: A set of standards for an entire country, usually including content standards, performance standards, and school standards

Norm Group: The group whose test performance is used to establish levels of performance on a standardized test

Norm-referenced Test: Test that measures the student's score with the average performance of all test takers

Objective Test: Test in which each question is stated in such a way that there is only one correct answer

Percentage Score: The percentage of correct responses on a test

Percentile Score: Proportion of other students' scores that equal or fall below a given student's score

Population: A complete set of students to which a set of test results will be generalized

Portfolio Assessment: Collecting children's work on an ongoing basis and examining it for evidence of growth

Raw Score: The number of correct responses on a test

Reliability: The consistency in test results or the degree to which a test's results actually measure what a student can do

Rubric: A scoring guide based on a scale for rating a group of students

Standardized Test: A test with specific procedures so that comparable measures may be made by testers in different geographic areas

Test Anxiety: Nervous energy felt by test takers; sharpens the mind

Test Bias: Tendency for a test to be unfair for students in some groups but not in others

Validity: The degree to which a test measures what it is designed to measure

Writing Assessment: A test in which students are asked to demonstrate writing abilities by actually writing in response to given prompts

Writing Prompt: A question or statement to which the test-taker is asked to respond

Overview of Testing Tips

- Read (or listen) to directions carefully.

- Follow all instructions, including icons.

- Read the entire question.

- Read all answer choices before picking one.

- Budget your time wisely.

- Do not spend too much time on any one question.

- Use all of the time provided; testing is not the same as a race.

- Pay close attention to how the question is written.

- Avoid making answer sheet errors.

- Skip hard questions, and answer the easy ones first.

- Use the process of elimination to find answers.

- Use logical reasoning to choose the best answer.

- When all else fails, guess.

- Answer all test questions.

- Think twice before changing an answer.

- Control test anxiety.

- Stay calm and focus on the task at hand.

Important Terms and Concepts

It might be helpful to review the following terms and concepts with the students prior to taking the practice tests.

Reading
comprehension
fantasy
fable
folk tale
poetry
alliteration
figurative language
characters
setting
context clues
proverbs
main idea/supporting details

Language Arts
synonym
antonym
analogy
palindrome
homophone
pronoun
topic sentence
supporting details
syllables
combining sentences
subject
predicate
capitalization
punctuation
web addresses (zones)
encyclopedias
dictionaries
libraries
Standard English
table of contents
glossary
maps, map key
webs

Math
symmetry
congruent
intersect
least common multiple
diameter
radius
volume
place value
Roman numerals
multiples
average
measurement
stopwatch
thermometer
addition
subtraction
multiplication
division
mathematician
less than
greater than
equal to
area
perimeter
fraction
simplest form
line
grid

Science
decomposers
fossil fuel
eclipse
buoyancy
carnivore
chlorophyll
food chain
herbivore
omnivore

photosynthesis
learned behavior
instinct
density
gravity
mass
volume
weight
planet
probe
rocky planet
frozen planet
telescope

Social Studies:

History and Culture
multicultural
continent
country
region
famous explorers
famous monuments
time line
Lewis and Clark
Trail of Tears
astronauts
charts, maps, grids, graphs
compass rose
Pearl Harbor
Twin Towers
United Nations
Wright Brothers
Thurgood Marshall
Neil Armstrong
Sally Ride
John Glenn
Condoleezza Rice
Colin Powell
Martin Luther King, Jr.

Important Terms and Concepts (cont.)

Civics, Government, Economics

goods
services
economy
consumer
producer
supply
demand
democracy
dictatorship
monarchy
Bill of Rights
Declaration of Independence
U.S. Constitution
legislative branch
executive branch
judicial branch
Senate
House of Representatives
governor
mayor
commander-in-chief
Ellis Island
Angel Island
immigrants

Geography

landforms
landmarks
maps, charts, graphs, grids
political map
topographical map
population map
climate map
resource map
states
regions
directions
major rivers
Amazon
Rio Grande
Gulf of Mexico
Caribbean Sea

Hi! Look for me! Whenever you see me, I'll give you some testing tip to help with your test-taking skills.

Filling Out the Answer Sheet

The first thing you will do during standardized testing is to correctly fill out your answer sheet. Below is an example of an answer sheet. The circles must be filled in for every box, so for empty boxes, fill in the empty circles. Use a No. 2 pencil, so the computer can score your answer sheet. Fill in your circles completely, and fill in only one for each question. If you erase an answer, be sure that you erase it completely before filling in your new choice. The computer will mark wrong any question that seems to have more than one choice marked. Erase all stray pencil marks on the page.

Practice filling out this sample form with your name. Print your name in the boxes at the top. Then darken the circle for that letter in the column under each letter. For blank spaces, darken the blank circles.

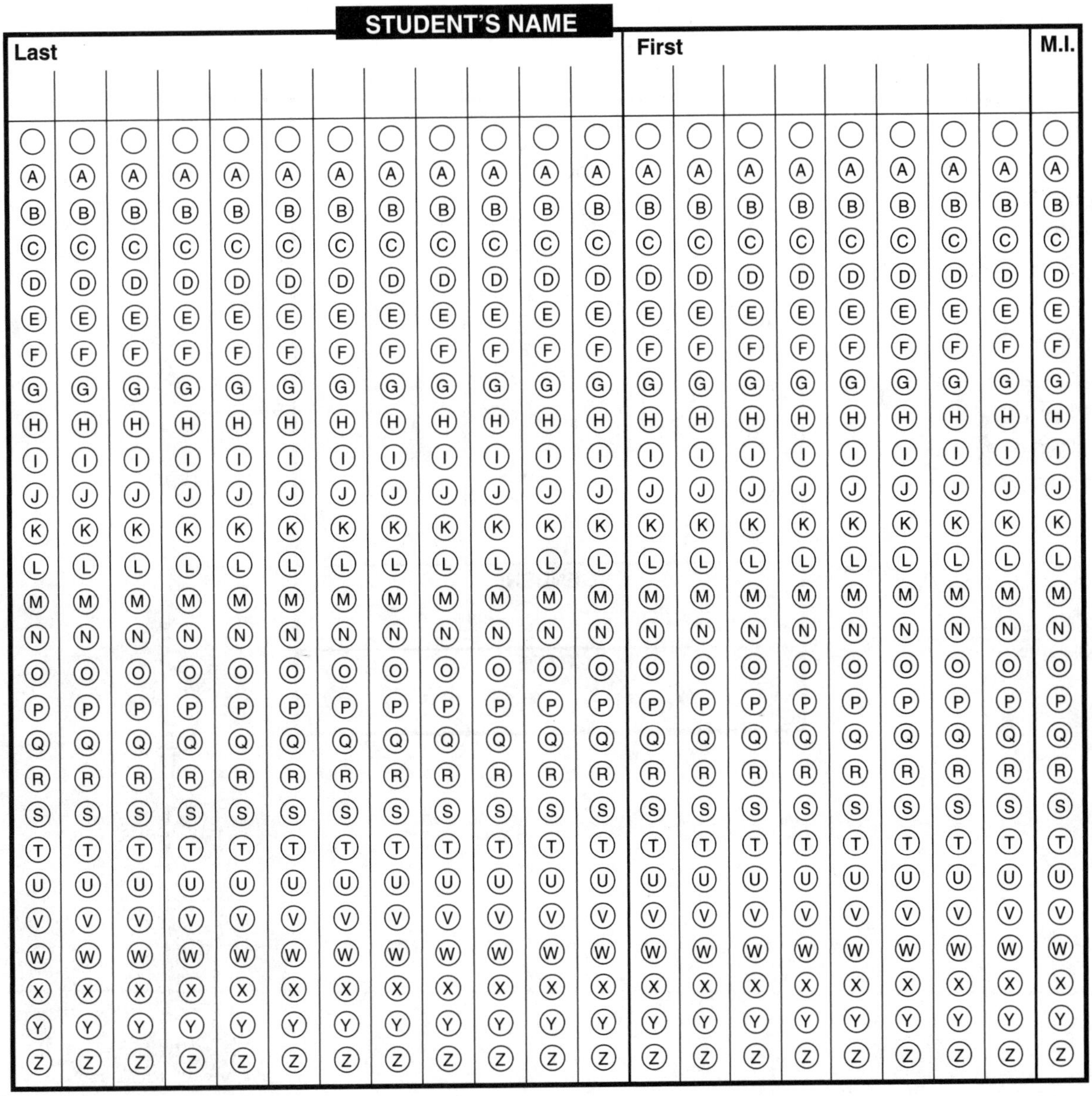

STUDENT'S NAME

Last   First   M.I.

(Answer sheet grid with circles labeled A through Z for each name column)

Filling Out the Answer Sheet (cont.)

Practice filling out this sample form with your birth date, gender, and grade. Print your teacher's name, school name, and district in the boxes at the top. Then darken the circles for your birth date, gender, and grade.

TEACHER
SCHOOL
DISTRICT

BIRTH DATE

Month	Day		Year	
Jan ○	⓪ ⓪		⓪	⓪
Feb ○	① ①			①
Mar ○	② ②			②
Apr ○	③ ③			③
May ○	④			④
Jun ○	⑤			⑤
Jul ○	⑥			⑥
Aug ○	⑦		⑦	⑦
Sep ○	⑧		⑧	⑧
Oct ○	⑨		⑨	⑨
Nov ○				
Dec ○				

GENDER

○ Female   ○ Male

GRADE

① ② ③ ④ ⑤ ⑥

Helpful Reading Strategies

Test Tips

1. Read <u>all</u> directions carefully.
2. Be sure you understand the directions.
3. Read <u>all</u> answer choices before choosing one.
4. Format changes may <u>not</u> signal a change in directions; don't be tricked.
5. Look for the key words in the directions.
6. Skip difficult items and come back to them.
7. Read back over your test to be sure you answered all questions.
8. If you aren't sure which answer is correct, take your best guess.

Reading Strategies

★ When reading comprehension is tested, the questions are testing your ability to read for details and to find meaning in the text.

★ When you are looking for the main idea of a selection, look at the first sentence, the last sentence, or the title. These usually provide a good clue as to the main idea.

★ When the directions say choose the *"most important idea,"* or *"the main problem,"* remember that there is probably more than one right answer. You need to look for the BEST answer.

★ When you are trying to figure out a vocabulary word from context, replace the word with the answer and see if it fits.

★ Watch out for negatives. Some questions say, *"which of the following **is not** true?"*. You are looking for the one that is wrong (false).

★ Use context clues to figure out words or ideas you don't understand.

★ Word-meaning questions test your vocabulary and your ability to figure out unfamiliar words.

Name: _Scan_

Date: _____

UNIT ONE: READING

Lesson One: Vocabulary

Directions: For questions 1–5, look for the word that means the *same* or *almost the same* as the underlined word.

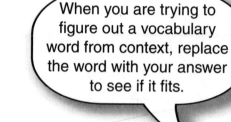

When you are trying to figure out a vocabulary word from context, replace the word with your answer to see if it fits.

1. The colorful balloon was right <u>above</u> her head.
   - A. near
   - B. below
   - C. over
   - D. on

2. Chad decided to <u>choose</u> soccer instead of football.
   - A. reject
   - B. select
   - C. play
   - D. watch

3. Peggy <u>made</u> a lovely bouquet of roses for her wedding.
   - A. created
   - B. bought
   - C. destroyed
   - D. threw

4. I was surprised by how <u>strong</u> the child was.
   - A. pretty
   - B. loud
   - C. nice
   - D. powerful

5. The fifth grade cleared the <u>vacant</u> lot to plant a garden.
   - A. messy
   - B. neighboring
   - C. full
   - D. empty

Directions: For questions 6–10, choose the word that means the *opposite* of the underlined word.

6. Sasha wanted <u>different</u> band uniforms.
   - A. colorful
   - B. the same
   - C. red
   - D. newer

7. My dad <u>repaired</u> the leaky faucet.
   - A. broke
   - B. fixed
   - C. examined
   - D. pulled

8. "<u>Push</u> harder!" Ravi yelled at the moving man.
   - A. move
   - B. row
   - C. shove
   - D. pull

Name: _Dean_____   Date: _____

Lesson One: Vocabulary (cont.)

9. Walker blinked at the <u>brilliant</u> light.
    A. dim   C. shiny
    B. bright   D. yellow

10. Frances <u>caught</u> the fly ball in the last inning.
    A. brought   C. threw
    B. hit   D. dropped

Word-meaning questions test your vocabulary and your ability to figure out unfamiliar words.

Directions: For questions 11–15, choose the word whose meaning fits both sentences.

11. Climb _____ the ladder quickly.
    She put fifty dollars _____ on the big-screen television at Wal-Mart.

    A. up   C. over
    B. down   D. around

12. Gerry taught us to swim with even _____.
    Nicholas paints with large, broad _____.

    A. strides   C. strokes
    B. movements   D. brushes

13. A mule is a _____ between a horse and a donkey.
    Don't _____ the street without the safety patrol boy.

    A. cross   C. trip
    B. block   D. run

14. The lighthouse is on the highest _____ of the island.
    There is no _____ in crying about it now.

    A. end   C. edge
    B. point   D. reason

3

Name: _Deany_____ Date: _____

Lesson One: Vocabulary (cont.)

15. Lloyd and Gabriella looked _____ after riding the roller coaster.
    Cows grazed in the _____ meadows.

    A. pale
    B. ripe
    C. grassy
    D. green

Directions: For questions 16–20, decide which modern word comes from the original word.

---

16. Which word comes from two Greek words that mean "river horse"?
    A. hippopotamus
    B. zebra
    C. stallion
    D. pony

17. Which word is probably short for *fiddle-faddle*, an old word meaning "nonsense."
    A. fair
    B. false
    C. fad
    D. foolish

18. Which word comes from an old English word that meant "to use oars"?
    A. boat
    B. dip
    C. paddle
    D. row

19. Which word is named after *Hamburg*, a large city in northern Germany?
    A. hamburger
    B. hamlet
    C. hammer
    D. hamper

20. Which word comes from an Arabic word meaning "earthen pot"?
    A. can
    B. jar
    C. javelin
    D. jute

Name: _Sean_   Date: _____

Lesson One: Vocabulary (cont.)

Directions: For questions 21–25, choose the word that finishes the analogy.

---

21. *Aunt* is to *niece* as *uncle* is to _____.
    A. cousin
    B. nephew
    C. son
    D. daughter

Skip difficult items and come back to them later.

22. *Bear* is to *cub* as *kangaroo* is to _____.
    A. bunny
    B. pup
    C. squab
    D. joey

23. *Roar* is to lion as _____ is to *turkey.*
    A. gobble
    B. squawk
    C. meow
    D. peep

24. *Leaf* is to tree as _____ is to *flower.*
    A. pistil
    B. stamen
    C. petal
    D. stem

25. _____ is to *computer* as *pencil* is to *paper.*
    A. disk
    B. keyboard
    C. monitor
    D. mouse

Name: _Sean_____ Date: _____

Lesson One: Vocabulary (cont.)

Directions: Read the paragraph. Then choose the word that best completes each blank in the paragraph.

Did you ever ___26___ why coins are round instead of square or some other shape? Well, the round shape makes it easy for banks to ___27___ them into rolls. Also, the round shape helps ___28___ coins made of gold or other ___29___ metals. Crooks have a harder time cutting or ___30___ off parts of a round coin before spending it.

Use context clues to figure out words or ideas you don't understand.

26. A. know   C. realize
    B. recall   D. wonder

27. A. swap   C. distribute
    B. wrap   D. clean

28. A. distribute   C. protect
    B. conceal   D. defend

29. A. valuable   C. mighty
    B. strong   D. major

30. A. cleaning   C. scraping
    B. melting   D. slashing

Review

1. When you are trying to figure out a vocabulary word from context, replace the word with your answer and see if it fits.
2. Word-meaning questions test your ability to figure out unfamiliar words.
3. Skip difficult items and come back to them later.
4. Use context clues to figure out words or ideas that you don't understand.

Thesaurus

Language Arts

GRAMMAR

Name: _____ Date: _____

UNIT ONE: READING

Lesson Two: Word Analysis

> **Directions:** For questions 1–5, choose the phrase that is closest to the meaning of the proverb.

Proverbs are old, wise sayings that are generally believed to be true.

1. **Everything has its price.** (American)
   A.   Nothing is free.
   B.   Things cost a lot of money.
   C.   Money is important to happiness.
   D.   You have to have money to buy things.

2. **Burn a candle at both ends, and it will not last long.** (Scottish)
   A.   To save money, don't burn a candle at both ends.
   B.   If you do too much, you'll burn yourself out.
   C.   If you say "yes" and "no," you'll burn out.
   D.   The candle is not made to burn at both ends.

If you aren't sure which answer is correct, take your best guess.

3. **Beauty is but skin deep.** (English)
   A.   Beauty on the outside doesn't mean beauty on the inside.
   B.   Beauty is worth taking care of.
   C.   It is important to take care of your skin.
   D.   To be beautiful costs money.

4. **One door is locked, but another is wide open.** (Russian)
   A.   If the door is locked, you have to have a key.
   B.   We often miss opportunities because the door is locked.
   C.   Don't leave the window open if you lock the door.
   D.   When the way you want to go isn't available, look for another way.

5. **To blame is easy, to do better is difficult.** (German)
   A.   Blaming others is not good.
   B.   You must take responsibility for yourself.
   C.   It's easier to blame someone else than to solve the problem yourself.
   D.   Some people do nothing but blame others.

Name: _____ Date: _____

Lesson Two: Word Analysis (cont.)

Directions: Read each sentence. Look for the words that have the *same* or *nearly the same* meaning as the underlined words.

6. The winter wrapped its <u>icy breath</u> around the village.
   A. snow
   B. freezing temperatures
   C. cold, cold wind
   D. chilly air

7. During the drill, she was <u>as cool as a cucumber</u>.
   A. not hot
   B. calm
   C. frightened
   D. frigid

8. Thornton had <u>butterflies in his stomach</u> before his piano recital.
   A. nervous energy
   B. insects in his stomach
   C. was sick to his stomach
   D. colorful wings tattooed on his stomach

9. In the moonlight, the dead tree <u>was a skeleton</u>.
   A. scary
   B. looked like bare bones
   C. invisible
   D. hollow

10. The girls spent a <u>dreamy</u> afternoon sprawled on the raft in the lake.
    A. fanciful
    B. vague
    C. wonderful
    D. drowsy

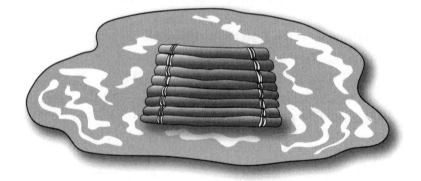

Name: _____   Date: _____

Lesson Two: Word Analysis (cont.)

> **Directions:** For questions 11–15, choose the best answer for each question.

Palindromes are words or sentences that are spelled the same forward or backward.

11. Which of these is *not* a palindrome?
    A. mom
    B. dad
    C. noon
    D. boat

12. Which of these sentences is a palindrome?
    A. Was it a rat I saw?
    B. Isn't it a rat I saw?
    C. Madam, I saw a rat.
    D. Bob did kayak with Dad.

Homophones are two words that sound the same but have different meanings and are usually spelled differently.

13. Which of these words are homophones?
    A. record, copy
    B. write, rite
    C. read, write
    D. meet, met

14. Which of these words are homophones?
    A. bank, slope
    B. rink, rank
    C. wrap, rap
    D. suspect, suspicious

15. Which word does *not* have a homophone?
    A. principle
    B. great
    C. bow
    D. hot

> Watch out for negatives. Some questions ask you "which is *not* true/correct/an example of." In this case, you are looking for the one that is wrong (false).

Name: _____   Date: _____

Lesson Two: Word Analysis (cont.)

Directions: For questions 16–25, choose the correct word for each sentence.

16. Whenever there is work to be done, the children _____.
    A.   disobey
    B.   disappear
    C.   disappoint
    D.   discredit

Read all directions carefully.

17. Gail had to _____ her paragraph.
    A.   rewind
    B.   rearrange
    C.   repeat
    D.   rewrite

18. The plant was so _____, it took up all the space.
    A.   overgrown
    B.   overlay
    C.   overrun
    D.   overdress

19. We met at _____ in the woods with our flashlights.
    A.   midpoint
    B.   midsummer
    C.   midnight
    D.   midday

20. The students complained that Mrs. Wilson was _____.
    A.   untouched
    B.   unfair
    C.   uneven
    D.   unraveled

Read all answers before choosing one.

21. Kenny said he was so smart because of his good _____.
    A.   rejection
    B.   election
    C.   collection
    D.   education

Name: _____ Date: _____

Lesson Two: Word Analysis (cont.)

22. The soldier's _____ comments put the troops at ease.
   A. humorous   C. courageous
   B. dangerous   D. nervous

23. It was well known that this was the best restaurant in the _____.
   A. adulthood   C. brotherhood
   B. neighborhood   D. boyhood

24. Mr. Levan always wore the _____ neckties.
   A. cleanest   C. widest
   B. tightest   D. farthest

25. _____ the little girl waited in the dentist's office for her
   mother.
   A. Sadly,   C. Attentively,
   B. Swiftly,   D. Patiently,

> Format changes often do not signal changes in directions.

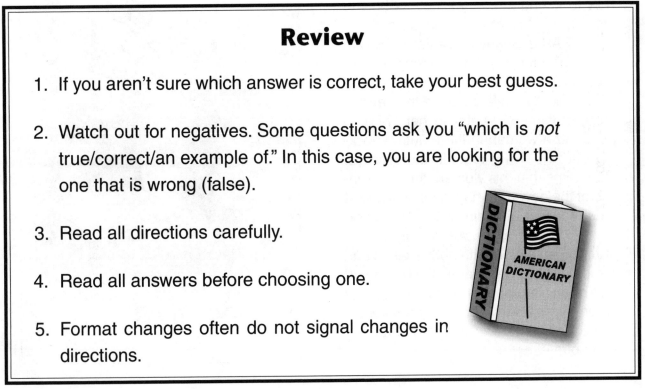

Review

1. If you aren't sure which answer is correct, take your best guess.

2. Watch out for negatives. Some questions ask you "which is *not* true/correct/an example of." In this case, you are looking for the one that is wrong (false).

3. Read all directions carefully.

4. Read all answers before choosing one.

5. Format changes often do not signal changes in directions.

Name: _____ Date: _____

UNIT ONE: READING

Lesson Three: Comprehension

Directions: Read the story, and then answer questions 1–5.

[1] Anne Bonny is probably the best-known female pirate. [2] She took what she wanted from the world and never apologized. [3] Anne was born in Ireland but moved shortly after with her family to South Carolina. [4] There she often masqueraded as a boy on her father's large plantation.

[5] When her marriage at sixteen didn't work out, she met a handsome rogue named Calico Jack Rackham and went to sea with him. [6] Calico Jack knew how to spend money as well as how to steal it, and this fit Anne's lifestyle.

[7] Anne Bonny was a fiery lass with a very bad temper. [8] As a young girl, rumor had it that Anne killed a servant woman with a knife because the servant made her mad. [9] Later in her life, she punched a woman in the mouth, knocking out two of her teeth in the process. [10] It seems that this woman, the sister-in-law of the governor, had insulted Anne at a ball she was attending with Calico Jack.

[11] As a pirate, Anne was just as fierce. [12] An expert with both a pistol and a rapier, Anne was fearless in battle and was often a member of the boarding party when a prize was about to be taken. [13] Anne Bonny was as dangerous as any male pirate!

Name: _____   Date: _____

Lesson Three: Comprehension (cont.)

1. Where was Anne Bonny born?
   A.   South Carolina
   B.   The Caribbean
   C.   Ireland
   D.   Scotland

2. Which of these events supports the idea that Anne had a bad temper?
   A.   She ran away with Calico Jack.
   B.   She punched a woman at a party.
   C.   She went to sea as a pirate.
   D.   none of these

3. In sentence 5, what does the word <u>rogue</u> mean?
   A.   a <u>young</u> man
   B.   a <u>cowardly</u> man
   C.   a <u>beautiful</u> man
   D.   a <u>tricky</u> man

4. In sentence 12, what does the word <u>rapier</u> mean?
   A.   knife
   B.   rifle
   C.   sword
   D.   blade

5. In sentence 10, to whom does the pronoun <u>she</u> refer?
   A.   Anne
   B.   the governor's sister-in-law
   C.   the governor
   D.   none of these

Reading comprehension tests your ability to read for details and to find meaning in text.

Name: _____ Date: _____

Lesson Three: Comprehension (cont.)

[1] One of the most popular fantasy characters is the leprechaun. Leprechauns are ugly little creatures with pointed ears. [2] They are about two to three feet tall—about the size of a kindergarten student.

[3] They have a mischievous glint in their eyes and tend to hide behind bushes and hedgerows. [4] Leprechauns move very, very fast, which is why it is impossible for humans to catch them. [5] Leprechauns avoid contact with humans and think they are stupid, foolish creatures.

6. Which of these is a definition for fantasy?
   A. not real
   B. real
   C. living in the past
   D. fable

When you are looking for the main idea, look at the first and last sentences and the title. These usually provide good clues.

7. Leprechauns don't like humans because
   A. humans are slow and dim.
   B. humans are real, and leprechauns aren't.
   C. humans are stupid and foolish.
   D. humans want to steal the leprechaun's gold.

8. Which of these is another word for mischievous (sentence 3)?
   A. hateful
   B. impish
   C. hurtful
   D. damaging

9. From this paragraph, what could you conclude about why leprechauns hide behind bushes and hedgerows?
   A. They are short enough not to be seen.
   B. They can jump out and scare humans.
   C. They don't want to be caught by humans.
   D. There is nowhere else to hide.

10. Which of these statements is true about fantasy?
    A. Fantasy takes place in the past.
    B. Fantasy has unexplainable magic.
    C. Fantasy is based on scientific events.
    D. All of these are true.

Name: _____ Date: _____

Lesson Three: Comprehension (cont.)

Directions: Read the narrative about armadillos, and then answer questions 11–15.

11. What is the main idea of this narrative?
    A. Armadillos are an endangered species.
    B. Armadillos can wreck a farmer's fields.
    C. Armadillos are interesting animals.
    D. Armadillos dig their way out of danger.

12. Which one of these is a reason an armadillo digs?
    A. for food and shelter
    B. to irritate farmers
    C. animal instinct
    D. to locate dead animals

13. What is meant by an "endangered species"?
    A. an animal that is gradually dying out
    B. an animal that destroys its young
    C. an animal that is over-hunted
    D. an animal that has migrated to another area

14. What is the topic sentence of paragraph 3?
    A. Armadillos are strong animals.
    B. Armadillos are built to dig.
    C. Armadillos have bad teeth.
    D. Armadillos can roll themselves into a ball.

15. From this narrative, you can tell that the author
    A. distrusts and dislikes armadillos.
    B. knows a lot about armadillos.
    C. lives in Texas.
    D. finds armadillos very interesting.

[1] Armadillos are an amazing endangered species and originate from South America. Contrary to popular belief, they are not rodents, they are not marsupials, and they are not related to opossums. However, they are mammals. There are actually twenty different kinds of armadillos.

[2] Armadillos have shells made of true bone covering their backs. Most armadillos have bony rings or plates that protect their tails. Because their backs are covered with bone, armadillos are not very flexible. One kind of armadillo, however, can roll itself into a ball.

[3] Armadillos are built to dig. They have short, strong legs that are well-suited to rapid digging, either for food or for shelter. They have strong claws that they use to help in digging or to tear apart rotting wood to find food such as grubs, ants, or beetles. Many armadillos also eat bits of flesh from dead animals if they can find them. If all else fails, most armadillos will eat plants, often wreaking havoc on farmers' fields.

[4] Because small bugs and soft plants are not too difficult to chew, armadillos do not have very complicated teeth. They have lost all their molars over time, and the teeth they have left are peg-shaped. Their teeth do not have the hard white enamel coating that protects the teeth of other mammals.

Name: _____ Date: _____

Lesson Three: Comprehension (cont.)

Directions: Read the poem to the left, and then answer questions 16–20.

Humanity
by Elma Stuckey

If I am blind and need someone
To keep me safe from harm,
It matters not the race to me
Of the one who takes my arm.

If I am saved from drowning
As I grasp and grope,
I will not stop to see the face
Of the one who throws the rope.

Or if out on some battlefield
I'm falling faint and weak,
The one who gently lifts me up
May any language speak.

We sip the water clear and cool,
No matter the hand that gives it.
A life that's lived worthwhile and fine,
What matters the one who lives it?

---

16. Why does the poet call her poem *Humanity*?

    A. because it's about what makes us human
    B. because people are just people
    C. because kindness and concern for others is important for all people
    D. because she couldn't think of a better title

17. From this poem, you can tell that the word grope in line 6 means

    A. to feel one's way.
    B. to clutch closely.
    C. to complain loudly.
    D. to fumble around.

18. What does the poet mean in the last two lines of the poem?

    A. A good life is a good life, no matter race, color, gender, or religion.
    B. Our similarities are more important than our differences.
    C. Race, gender, and religion are not important to living a good life.
    D. Why do our differences matter?

19. In which order did the events in the poem happen?

    A. saving, offering, carrying, helping
    B. helping, saving, carrying, offering
    C. offering, helping, carrying, saving
    D. carrying, saving, helping, offering

20. Which of these words from the poem is an example of alliteration (sounds that are repeated)?

    A. safe from harm
    B. faint and weak
    C. grasp and grope
    D. sip the water

Name: _____ Date: _____

Lesson Three: Comprehension (cont.)

Directions: Read the story, and then answer questions 21–30.

Once there was a man in a small village who was a terrible gossip. He always had stories to tell about his friends and neighbors. Even if he didn't know someone, he still found stories to tell about them.

With the coming of the New Year, the man thought he would make a resolution to stop gossiping, so he went to the rabbi. "Rabbi," he said, "I feel bad about the gossip and rumors I've spread, and I want to make amends. Please tell me what to do to atone."

The rabbi thought for a few minutes and then said, "I'll tell you what you must do, if you promise to do exactly what I tell you to do ... and no questions asked!" The man promised to do exactly what the rabbi told him and to do it without asking any questions.

The rabbi told the man to go into the marketplace and buy a fresh chicken, pluck all of the feathers off the chicken, and bring it to the rabbi as fast as he could.

Well, the man could not imagine what the rabbi wanted with the chicken, but since he had promised not to ask any questions, he took off for the marketplace as fast as his legs could run. When he got to the market, he bought the best, plumpest chicken he could find. On his way back to the rabbi's house, he plucked the feathers off the chicken as he ran. When he got to the rabbi's door, not a single feather remained on the chicken.

Out of breath, he gently handed the chicken to the rabbi who turned it over and over looking for feathers. Finally, he turned to the man and said, "Good work. Now bring me the feathers. "

"Rabbi," gasped the man, "how can I do that? The wind must have carried all those feathers far, far away. I could never find them all!"

"That's true," said the rabbi. "And that's how it is with gossip and rumors. One rumor can fly to many places, and how could you retrieve it? Better not to speak gossip in the first place!"

And he sent the man home to apologize to all of his neighbors.

Name: _____ Date: _____

Lesson Three: Comprehension (cont.)

21. Why did the man go to the rabbi?
    A.   He was a man of faith.
    B.   He wanted to stop gossiping.
    C.   He wanted to get away from his wife.
    D.   The rabbi invited him.

22. Who are the two main characters?
    A.   the rabbi and the man who gossiped
    B.   the chicken and the rabbi
    C.   the man and his neighbors
    D.   the chicken and the neighbors

23. Where does this story take place?
    A.   It doesn't say.
    B.   in the marketplace
    C.   in a small village
    D.   in the rabbi's house

Look for key words in directions.

24. What is another word for <u>resolution</u> in the second paragraph?
    A.   intention
    B.   statement
    C.   idea
    D.   opinion

Be sure you under-stand all directions.

25. How do you think the man felt at the end of the story?
    A.   happy because he was free
    B.   determined to change his behavior
    C.   embarrassed because he had to apologize
    D.   relieved because the rabbi forgave him

26. In the last sentence of paragraph 2 is the word <u>atone</u>. What does it mean?
    A.   cause problems
    B.   reconcile
    C.   pay back
    D.   make amends

27. How did the rabbi teach the man a lesson?
    A.   He demonstrated the spread of rumors with the spread of the feathers.
    B.   He spread gossip and rumors about the man.
    C.   He wrote the man a letter telling him to stop it.
    D.   He told all the neighbors to avoid the man.

Name: _____ Date: _____

Lesson Three: Comprehension (cont.)

28. This story is an example of a
    A. fairy tale.
    B. folk tale.
    C. legend.
    D. myth.

29. What would be the best title for this story?
    A. The Rabbi
    B. The Village
    C. The Gossip
    D. Learning a Lesson

30. What lesson can be learned from this story?
    A. Gossip and spreading rumors is a nasty behavior.
    B. Once a rumor or gossip starts, it's impossible to stop it.
    C. Rumors, like feathers, fly through the air.
    D. Keep your New Year's resolutions.

> When the directions say to choose the most important idea, you know there is probably more than one right answer. Choose the BEST answer.

> Read back over your test to see if you answered all of the questions.

Review

1. When you are looking for the main idea, look at the first and last sentences and the title. These usually provide good clues.
2. Look for key words in directions.
3. Be sure you understand all directions.
4. When the directions say to choose the most important idea, you know there is probably more than one right answer. Choose the BEST answer.
5. Read back over your test to see if you answered all of the questions.

Thesaurus
Language Arts
GRAMMAR

Helpful Language Strategies

Test Tips

1. The most important test tip is to be <u>confident</u>.
2. Read all maps, charts, and graphs carefully.
3. Decide what you think the answer is before reading the choices.
4. Read all choices before answering each question.
5. Choose your answers carefully. More than one choice may *seem* correct.
6. Eliminate choices that you know are wrong, and then guess.
7. Make sure you fill in the correct circle on your answer sheet.
8. If you <u>have</u> to change an answer, be sure you erase your mistake <u>completely</u>.

Language Strategies

★ Language tests usually include questions about spelling, grammar, punctuation, and capitalization.

★ Standard English is the kind of language you read in books and hear on the news.

★ When in doubt, say the answer choices softly to yourself. Which one *sounds* correct?

★ Use context clues to figure out tough questions.

★ The purpose of punctuation is to signal meaning to the reader.

★ If you are not sure of the spelling, try writing the word out on scratch paper. Which word *looks* right?

★ When sentences are combined, make sure the meaning of the sentence is not changed.

Name: _____   Date: _____

UNIT TWO: LANGUAGE

Lesson One: Mechanics

> **Directions:** Choose the letter that shows the correct way to divide the word into syllables.

1. A.   jewelry
    B.   jewel - ry
    C.   jew - el - ry
    D.   je - wel - ry

2. A.   peach
    B.   pe - a - ch
    C.   pea - ch
    D.   pe - ach

3. A.   bumpier
    B.   bum - pier
    C.   bump - ier
    D.   bump - i - er

4. A.   monument
    B.   mon - u - ment
    C.   monu - ment
    D.   mon - ument

5. A.   quiet
    B.   qui - et
    C.   qu - iet
    D.   quie - t

6. A.   flipper
    B.   flipp - er
    C.   flip - per
    D.   fli - pper

7. A.   recycling
    B.   re - cycl - ing
    C.   re - cy - cling
    D.   recy - cling

8. A.   vacation
    B.   va - ca - tion
    C.   vac - a - tion
    D.   vaca - tion

9. A.   recorder
    B.   rec - or - der
    C.   re - cord - er
    D.   re - cor - der

10. A.   wipe
    B.   wi - pe
    C.   wip - e
    D.   w - ipe

Language tests usually include questions about spelling, grammar, punctuation, and capitalization.

Name: _____ Date: _____

Lesson One: Mechanics (cont.)

Directions: Choose the correct spelling of each word.

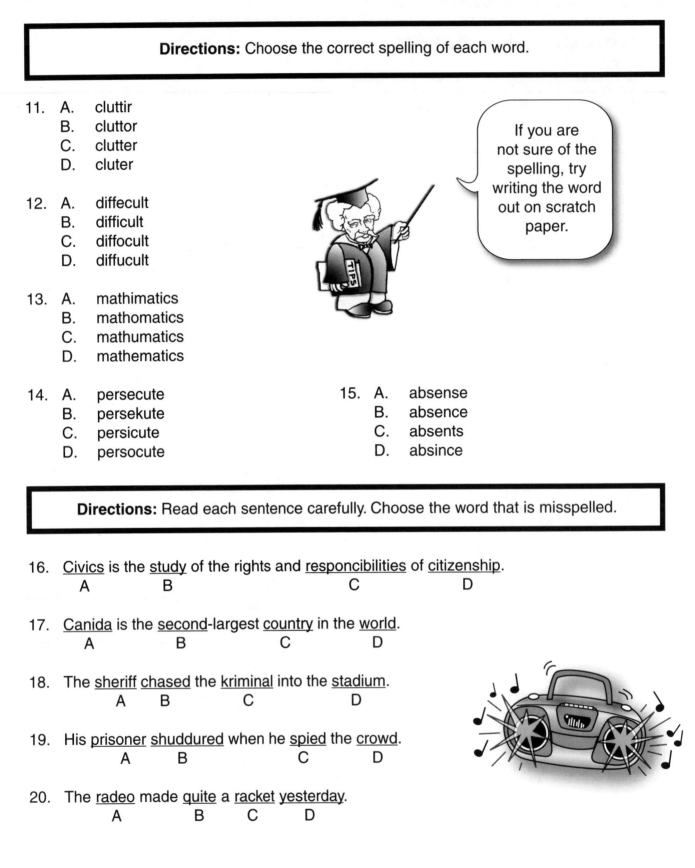

11. A. cluttir
    B. cluttor
    C. clutter
    D. cluter

12. A. diffecult
    B. difficult
    C. diffocult
    D. diffucult

13. A. mathimatics
    B. mathomatics
    C. mathumatics
    D. mathematics

14. A. persecute
    B. persekute
    C. persicute
    D. persocute

15. A. absense
    B. absence
    C. absents
    D. absince

If you are not sure of the spelling, try writing the word out on scratch paper.

Directions: Read each sentence carefully. Choose the word that is misspelled.

---

16. <u>Civics</u> is the <u>study</u> of the rights and <u>responcibilities</u> of <u>citizenship</u>.
    A   B   C   D

17. <u>Canida</u> is the <u>second</u>-largest <u>country</u> in the <u>world</u>.
    A   B   C   D

18. The <u>sheriff</u> <u>chased</u> the <u>kriminal</u> into the <u>stadium</u>.
    A   B   C   D

19. His <u>prisoner</u> <u>shuddured</u> when he <u>spied</u> the <u>crowd</u>.
    A   B   C   D

20. The <u>radeo</u> made <u>quite</u> a <u>racket</u> <u>yesterday</u>.
    A   B   C   D

Name: _____ Date: _____

Lesson One: Mechanics (cont.)

Directions: Choose the part of the sentence that contains an error in capitalization. If there are no mistakes, choose "D."

21. A. Part of the roof
    B. collapsed under
    C. the weight of the snow.
    D. no mistakes

22. A. the president
    B. clashed with the Senate
    C. over the tax bill.
    D. no mistakes

23. A. I would like to
    B. collect the Money
    C. you owe me.
    D. no mistakes

24. A. The cowboys fought
    B. the soldiers east
    C. of the red river.
    D. no mistakes

25. A. my birthday
    B. is on the last Monday
    C. in March.
    D. no mistakes

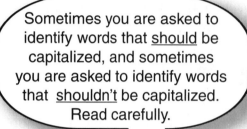

Sometimes you are asked to identify words that should be capitalized, and sometimes you are asked to identify words that shouldn't be capitalized. Read carefully.

Directions: Decide which punctuation mark, if any, is needed in each sentence.

26. The lunch money is on my desk
    A. .
    B. ?
    C. " "
    D. none

27. How is that word spelled
    A. .
    B. ?
    C. !
    D. none

Name: _____ Date: _____

Lesson One: Mechanics (cont.)

28. "Sisters Week will be in June," my three sisters decided.
    A.   Sister's
    B.   Sisters'
    C.   Sisters.
    D.   none

29. Wow you just won the art contest.
    A.   Wow. You
    B.   Wow? You
    C.   Wow! You
    D.   none

30. Barbie of course was late for school again.
    A.   Barbie of, course
    B.   Barbie of course,
    C.   Barbie, of, course,
    D.   Barbie, of course,

Directions: Choose the answer that shows the best capitalization and punctuation for the underlined part of the sentence.

The weather in <u>Portland Oregon</u> is often rainy.

31. A.   Portland, oregon
     B.   Portland Oregon,
     C.   Portland, Oregon,
     D.   portland, Oregon

The <u>Garage Sale</u> will be held on <u>Friday, Saturday and Sunday</u>

32. A.   garage sale
     B.   Garage sale
     C.   garage Sale
     D.   correct as it is

33. A.   Friday, Saturday, and Sunday
     B.   Friday, Saturday, and Sunday.
     C.   Friday, Saturday, and, Sunday.
     D.   correct as it is

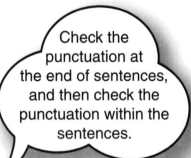

Check the punctuation at the end of sentences, and then check the punctuation within the sentences.

Name: _____ Date: _____

Lesson One: Mechanics (cont.)

Dear Aunt Jo

34. A. dear aunt jo,
    B. dear Aunt Jo
    C. Dear Aunt Jo,
    D. correct as it is

The most important test tip is to be confident!

"Tell Mrs. Greene <u>Ill be late,</u>" Zak said.

35. A. I'll be late"
    B. I'll be late."
    C. I'll be late,"
    D. correct as it is

Directions: Read each sentence carefully. Find the line with the mistake. If there is no mistake, then choose answer "D."

---

36. A. I heard that
    B. your going to
    C. go to Florida this summer.
    D. no mistake

37. A. "Pick up them
    B. soda bottles!"
    C. the mean man hollered.
    D. no mistake

38. A. Mary and Steve
    B. have went to the
    C. apple orchard.
    D. no mistake

39. A. Me and you
    B. are going to
    C. Raging Rivers.
    D. no mistake

40. A. The band played
    B. loudly, right were
    C. the baby slept.
    D. no mistake

41. A. I am grateful.
    B. My mom is grateful.
    C. My dad is gratefulest.
    D. no mistake

42. A. Your son
    B. did a good job
    C. fixing the computer.
    D. no mistake

43. A. Its only raining
    B. on one side
    C. of the street!
    D. no mistake

44. A. Slowly, the children
    B. filed to there
    C. auditorium seats.
    D. no mistake

45. A. The teacher
    B. sat right hear
    C. next to me.
    D. no mistake

Name: _____   Date: _____

Lesson One: Mechanics (cont.)

Review

1. Language tests usually include questions about spelling, grammar, punctuation, and capitalization.

2. If you are not sure of the spelling, try writing the word out on scratch paper.

3. Sometimes you are asked to identify words that <u>should</u> be capitalized, and sometimes you are asked to identify words that <u>shouldn't</u> be capitalized. Read carefully.

4. Check the punctuation at the end of sentences, and then check the punctuation within sentences.

5. The most important test tip is to be confident!

Name: _____   Date: _____

UNIT TWO: LANGUAGE

Lesson Two: Expression

Directions: Choose the correct word to complete the sentence.

1. _____ is the jacket I wanted.
   A. Their
   B. There
   C. They're
   D. They

Standard English is the kind of language you read in books and hear on the news.

2. Wesley's father told _____ a scary ghost story.
   A. us
   B. I
   C. myself
   D. we

3. Tell her _____ serious about the trip.
   A. your
   B. you
   C. you're
   D. yous

4. The man waited for the woman to _____ down.
   A. sat
   B. set
   C. sit
   D. sitted

5. Will you carry _____ boxes for me?
   A. these
   B. that
   C. this
   D. them

6. Kelly is _____ to figure skate.
   A. learned
   B. learn
   C. learning
   D. learner

Name: _____ Date: _____

Lesson Two: Expression (cont.)

Directions: Choose the word that best replaces the underlined word in each sentence.

---

7. That cute dog belongs to <u>Jill</u>.
   A. she
   B. her
   C. him
   D. it

8. Jill had <u>three dogs</u> in her yard.
   A. them
   B. their
   C. it
   D. him

9. Rick asked <u>Mark</u> if the dogs were for sale.
   A. he
   B. his
   C. him
   D. her

10. Lucy takes <u>Lucy's</u> job very seriously.
    A. his
    B. her
    C. it
    D. its

When in doubt, say the answer choices softly to yourself. Which one *sounds* correct?

Directions: Read each sentence carefully. Find the line with the mistake. If there is no mistake, then choose answer "D."

---

11. A. Earth is a
    B. planet that
    C. orbit the sun.
    D. no mistake

12. A. Eight other
    B. planet orbit
    C. the sun.
    D. no mistake

13. A. Most planets
    B. have moon
    C. orbiting them.
    D. no mistake

14. A. Our galaxy, the
    B. Milky Way, is one of
    C. many galaxy.
    D. no mistake

　　　　28

Name: _____ Date: _____

Lesson Two: Expression (cont.)

15. A.   Wasn't we lucky
    B.   to escape the
    C.   huge hurricane?
    D.   no mistake

16. A.   Do you
    B.   wanna go to
    C.   the mall on Tuesday?
    D.   no mistake

17. A.   Ira will never
    B.   guess who we
    C.   choosed for our captain.
    D.   no mistake

18. A.   Her and I have
    B.   been the best of
    C.   friends for years.
    D.   no mistake

19. A.   On our vacation,
    B.   Earl brung his
    C.   dirt bike.
    D.   no mistake

20. A.   My little brother is
    B.   very excited about
    C.   starting school.
    D.   no mistake

Directions: Choose the sentence that sounds best when you combine the two sentences.

---

21. The birthday cake was red and blue.
    The ice cream was white.

    A.   The birthday cake was red and blue, and the ice cream was white.
    B.   The white ice cream went with the red and blue birthday cake.
    C.   The birthday cake was red and blue, but the ice cream was white.
    D.   none of these

22. Two dogs chased the squirrels.
    Five children chased the dogs.

    A.   Two dogs and five children chased the squirrels.
    B.   While two dogs chased the squirrels, five children chased the dogs.
    C.   The squirrels were chased by two dogs, and the two dogs were chased by five children.
    D.   none of these

> When sentences are combined, make sure the meaning of the sentence is not changed.

Name: _____ Date: _____

Lesson Two: Expression (cont.)

23. Fay got lost at the carnival.
     Fay's brother got lost at the carnival.

     A.   Fay and her brother both got lost at the carnival.
     B.   At the carnival, Fay and Fay's brother got lost.
     C.   Lost, were Fay and her brother at the carnival.
     D.   none of these

24. My grandmother tripped on the bump in the sidewalk. She fell and broke her leg.

     A.   Grandmother tripped on the bump in the sidewalk and fell and broke her leg.
     B.   My grandmother broke her leg on the bump in the sidewalk when she tripped and fell.
     C.   When my grandmother tripped on the sidewalk, she fell and broke her leg.
     D.   none of these

25. Please tell me you'll come! Tell me you will! Tell me right now!

     A.   Right now please tell me you'll come!
     B.   You will come, please, right now!
     C.   Please tell me right now that you'll come!
     D.   Tell please now right come you!

Directions: Choose the simple subject in each sentence.

---

26. My dog, Harry, barks at the bad guys on television.
     A.   dog
     B.   dog, Harry
     C.   My dog, Harry
     D.   television

Decide what you think the answer is before reading the choices.

27. Upon entering the circus tent, the children's eyes began to sparkle.
     A.   children
     B.   tent
     C.   eyes
     D.   sparkle

28. Wendell's friends put a swimming pool in their backyard.
     A.   Wendell
     B.   friends
     C.   pool
     D.   backyard

Name: _____ Date: _____

Lesson Two: Expression (cont.)

29. Most of our trash goes to places called landfills.
    A. Most
    B. our
    C. places
    D. trash

30. Halle Berry and Denzel Washington both won top acting Oscars in 2002.
    A. Halle Berry
    B. Denzel Washington
    C. Oscars
    D. Halle Berry and Denzel Washington

31. Whooping cranes are an endangered species.
    A. Whooping
    B. cranes
    C. Whooping cranes
    D. species

Directions: Choose the simple predicate in each sentence.

---

32. Zip disks hold much more information than floppy disks.
    A. hold
    B. hold more
    C. hold more information
    D. disks

33. Computer technicians install and replace computer equipment.
    A. install
    B. replace
    C. install and replace
    D. computer

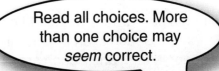

Read all choices. More than one choice may *seem* correct.

34. Caring for patients and helping doctors are two important responsibilities of nurses.
    A. caring
    B. helping
    C. caring and helping
    D. are

Name: _____　Date: _____

Lesson Two: Expression (cont.)

35. List the names and birthdays of your family members.
    A. List
    B. names
    C. your
    D. members

Directions: Read the paragraphs carefully, and then answer the questions.

> Miami Beach is a city in southeast Florida. It has miles of sandy beaches. It is famous for its Gold Coast strip of fashionable hotels, huge mansions, and recreational facilities. The beach is truly awesome! Many families play and swim along the shore with its white sand, palm trees, and clear blue water. Miami Beach is also an important resort and cruise center for the Caribbean.

36. The main idea of this paragraph is that
    A. Miami Beach would be a good place to vacation.
    B. there are many miles of sandy beaches in Miami Beach.
    C. there is much to see in Miami Beach.
    D. Miami Beach is in southeast Florida.

37. From this paragraph, you could conclude that
    A. Miami Beach is an important city in Florida.
    B. people in Miami Beach are nice.
    C. there is little water pollution in Miami Beach.
    D. the beach is a great place to vacation.

38. To what does the word *it* in sentence 2 refer?
    A. city
    B. miles
    C. Miami Beach
    D. beaches

Use context clues to figure out tough questions.

Name: _____ Date: _____

Lesson Two: Expression (cont.)

> In winter, black bears and grizzly bears curl up in dens and go to sleep. While hibernating, the bears get energy by burning the fat they stored in their bodies during the summer and fall. This body fat has to last until spring; so to save energy, the bears breathe more slowly and less often. During hibernation, their body temperature drops a few degrees below normal. They are, however, able to wake up in a hurry if they have to.

39. This paragraph explains how
    A. animals survive winter.
    B. bears hibernate in winter.
    C. bears store body fat.
    D. body fat is stored.

> Read all choices. More than one choice may *seem* correct.

40. Which one of these would be a good title for this paragraph?
    A. Bearzzzzzz
    B. Bears in Winter
    C. Sleepy Bears
    D. Winter Hibernation

41. From this paragraph, you might conclude that
    A. bears are fat in winter.
    B. bears get cold in winter.
    C. if disturbed, the bears *will* wake up.
    D. bears don't wake up until the snow melts.

42. Choose the sentence that best supports this topic sentence:

    Penguins hang out in big groups.

    A. Penguins live in the coldest place on Earth: Antarctica.
    B. Penguins molt (get a new coat of feathers).
    C. Penguin parents feed their babies by regurgitating fish.
    D. It is easier to find mates, protect the young, and keep warm in a crowd.

43. Choose the sentence that does *not* provide supporting details for this topic sentence:

    The southern tip of Florida is a beautiful, water-filled wilderness.

    A. Sawgrass, cypress trees, and mangrove swamps cover the slow-moving water.
    B. The Everglades gets over 60 inches of rain, mostly in the summer.
    C. You can see birds, butterflies, snakes, turtles, and alligators in the Everglades.
    D. Seminole Indians once lived in this area.

     33

Name: _____ Date: _____

Lesson Two: Expression (cont.)

> In 1912, the *Titanic* was the world's largest, fastest, and most luxurious ship, and it was thought to be unsinkable. However, the famous ocean liner struck an iceberg off the North American coast in the early hours of April 15. At first, the crew thought the damage was slight, but about two hours later, the ship plunged to the bottom of the Atlantic Ocean, and 1,500 people drowned. There had not been enough lifeboats for everyone. Many of those drowned were emigrants who had been planning to start a new life in the United States.

44. What would be a good title for this paragraph?
    A. The *Titanic*
    B. Sinking the Unsinkable
    C. Giant of the Ocean
    D. Bad Luck Lady

45. What does the word <u>luxurious</u> mean?
    A. splendid and comfortable
    B. large and roomy
    C. pleasing and prepared
    D. abundant and lush

Make sure you fill in the correct circle on your answer sheet!

Name: _____ Date: _____

Lesson Two: Expression (cont.)

Review

1. Standard English is the kind of language you read in books and hear on the news.

2. When in doubt, say the answer choices softly to yourself. Which one *sounds* correct?

3. When sentences are combined, make sure the meaning of the sentence is not changed.

4. Decide what you think the answer is before reading the choices.

5. Use context clues to figure out tough questions.

6. Read all choices. More than one choice may *seem* correct.

7. Make sure you fill in the correct circle on your answer sheet!

Name: _____ Date: _____

UNIT TWO: LANGUAGE

Lesson Three: Information Skills

Directions: Read the Michigan web carefully. Then answer questions 1–3.

G. History

A. Upper Penninsula

F. Water Wonderland

B. Capital

E. Automobiles

D. Famous Michiganders

C. Large Cities

1. Which city belongs on line B?
   A. Detroit
   B. Ann Arbor
   C. Lansing
   D. Grand Rapids

2. On which line does this information belong?

   Michigan is the only state that comes in two parts.

   A. A   B. B   C. C   D. D

3. On which line does this information belong?

   The Ojibwa, the Ottawa, and the Potawatomi Native Americans lived in Michigan.

   A. B   B. E   C. F   D. G

Name: _____ Date: _____

Lesson Three: Information Skills (cont.)

Directions: Read the paragraph about fish and amphibians, and then answer the questions.

Fish are vertebrates that live in the water and breathe oxygen through their gills. Fish are cold-blooded, which means that their body temperature stays the same as the water around them.

Amphibians are also vertebrates. Some live in water and some on land, but most start their lives in water. Amphibians absorb water and oxygen from the air directly through their skin. For this reason, they must keep their skin moist. Amphibians, like fish, are cold-blooded animals.

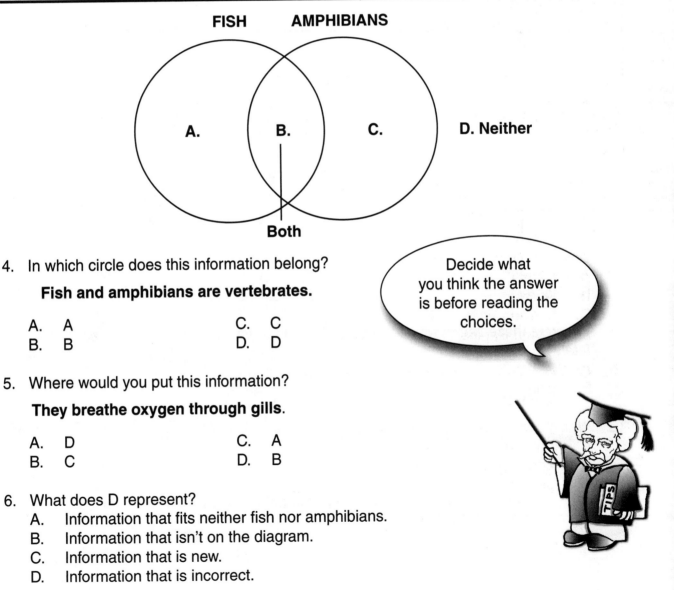

FISH   **AMPHIBIANS**

A.   **B.**   **C.**   **D. Neither**

Both

4. In which circle does this information belong?

    Fish and amphibians are vertebrates.

    A. A
    B. B
    C. C
    D. D

> Decide what you think the answer is before reading the choices.

5. Where would you put this information?

    They breathe oxygen through gills.

    A. D
    B. C
    C. A
    D. B

6. What does D represent?
    A. Information that fits neither fish nor amphibians.
    B. Information that isn't on the diagram.
    C. Information that is new.
    D. Information that is incorrect.

Name: _____ Date: _____

Lesson Three: Information Skills (cont.)

Directions: Read the paragraph. For each numbered blank 7–10, there is a list of words with the same number. Choose the word that best completes the meaning of the paragraph.

Chimpanzees are the most human looking of all the ___7___. Fully grown, they are about 3–6 feet tall and are able to ___8___ upright, although they usually walk on all fours, using their hands to help push themselves along. Chimps are found in the ___9___ of west and central Africa. They live in family groups and take good care of their young. Chimps are playful and intelligent animals. They can learn to talk in sign language and perform simple tasks.

Chimpanzees are among the ___10___ of all mammals. They scream and shriek, drum on trees, slap the ground, and keep up an almost constant hooting and muttering.

7. A. primates   C. animals
    B. apes   D. mammals

8. A. walk   C. glide
    B. swim   D. skate

9. A. sweaty jungle   C. majestic mountains
    B. dry deserts   D. tropical forests

10. A. nosiest   C. noisiest
    B. largest   D. strongest

11. Which of these words would *not* be on a dictionary page with the guide words *laser* and *lately*?
    A. last   C. latch
    B. launch   D. lasso

12. Which choice shows the words in correct alphabetical order?
    A. landscape, landlady, landmark, landslide
    B. landmark, landscape, landslide, landlady
    C. landlady, landmark, landslide, landscape
    D. landlady, landmark, landscape, landslide

Name: _____   Date: _____

Lesson Three: Information Skills (cont.)

13. If you wanted to find a synonym for <u>glow</u>, where would you look?
    A. dictionary
    B. encyclopedia
    C. thesaurus
    D. atlas

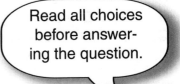

Read all choices before answering the question.

14. When reading your social studies book, you aren't sure of the definition of the <u>Prime Meridian</u>. Where would you look for the definition?
    A. table of contents
    B. index
    C. appendix
    D. glossary

15. Look at the website addresses. At which one would you look to find information about recent news events?
    A. <u>www.abcnews.go.com</u>
    B. <u>www.infoplease.com</u>
    C. <u>www.barnesandnoble.com</u>
    D. <u>www.angellove.com</u>

Directions: Use the drawing of the computer for questions 16–18.

---

16. What is number 6?
    A. keyboard
    B. disk drive
    C. mouse
    D. hard drive

17. If you wanted to use a CD on this computer, where would you put it?
    A. 3
    B. 5
    C. 4
    D. 7

18. What part of the computer do you use for word processing?
    A. 5   C. 7
    B. 3   D. 6

Lesson Three: Information Skills (cont.)

19. If you had a math question you wanted to ask an expert, which website would you use?
   A. Ask Professor Math email>maths@sbu.edu
   B. K–12 Explorer http://unite.ukans.edu
   C. Geometry Forum http://forum.swartmore.edu/
   D. NCTM http://www.nctm.org

> **Directions:** Examine the four website addresses and the chart, *Zones and What They Represent* for questions 20–23.

   1. www.nctm.org
   2. www.bn.com
   3. www.arizona.edu
   4. www.isbe.gov

ZONES AND WHAT THEY REPRESENT	
Zones	**Representation**
com	commercial organization
edu	educational organization or institution
mil	military-related site
net	network organization
org	professional group or organization
int	international organization or association
gov	government organization or agency
ca	name of a country (ca: Canada)

20. Which of these four websites belongs to a school or university?
   A. 1
   B. 2
   C. 3
   D. 4

21. Which of these four websites belongs to a national, state, or local government?
   A. 1
   B. 2
   C. 3
   D. 4

22. Which of these four websites belongs to a business?
   A. 1
   B. 2
   C. 3
   D. 4

23. Which of these four websites belongs to an organization or club?
   A. 1
   B. 2
   C. 3
   D. 4

Name: _____ Date: _____

Lesson Three: Information Skills (cont.)

Directions: Read the questions, and choose the best answer.

24. If you were writing a report on former President Ronald Reagan, which volume of the encyclopedia would you use?
    A. Ru – Sap
    B. Pan – Ro
    C. Min – Pam
    D. Ma – Mil

25. You find out that Reagan was born in Tampico, and since you don't know anything about Tampico, you decide to look it up. Which volume would you use?
    A. 9
    B. 10
    C. 11
    D. 12

26. Reagan graduated from Eureka College. What volume would you use to find information about the college?
    A. Co – Das
    B. Def – Fo
    C. Fu – Gi
    D. Ru – Sap

Name: _____ Date: _____

Lesson Three: Information Skills (cont.)

Directions: Use the table of contents to the right to answer questions 27–30.

27. On which page might you find some threats to biodiversity?
    A. 65
    B. 64
    C. 71
    D. 73

TABLE OF CONTENTS

28. On which page will you find information about the effects of global warming?
    A. 70
    B. 71
    C. 72
    D. 73

29. If you wanted to know what is made from recycled materials, on what page would you look?
    A. 64
    B. 69
    C. 70
    D. 73

30. Where would you find out the definition of a "biome"?
    A. 64
    B. 65
    C. 66
    D. 68

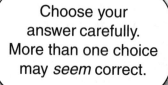

Choose your answer carefully. More than one choice may *seem* correct.

Name: _____   Date: _____

Lesson Three: Information Skills (cont.)

Directions: Study the map. Then answer questions 31–35.

31. On which side of the island is the Stingray City Sand Bar?
    A. North
    B. South
    C. East
    D. West

32. If you wanted to go to the northernmost city on this island, where would you go?
    A. Great Pedro Point
    B. Roger's Wreck Point
    C. Dolphin Point
    D. Hell

33. If you wanted to swim with the stingrays, what body of water would you be in?
    A. Pacific Ocean
    B. Caribbean Sea
    C. Persian Gulf
    D. Atlantic Ocean

34. What city is just north of Half Moon Bay?
    A. Blow Holes
    B. East Point
    C. Frank Sound
    D. Old Man Bay

35. If you wanted some fresh bread, where would you go for it?
    A. Turtle Farm
    B. George Town
    C. Hell
    D. Bodden Town

It's usually not a good idea to change your answers.

Name: _____ Date: _____

Lesson Three: Information Skills (cont.)

Directions: Which definition best matches the underlined word in each sentence?

36. The thermometer <u>reads</u> 89°.
    A. 2
    B. 3
    C. 4
    D. 5

37. My sister <u>read</u> my personal diary to her friend.
    A. 2
    B. 3
    C. 4
    D. 5

read *verb* 1. To understand the meaning of written or printed words. 2. To say aloud the words of something written or printed: *Our parents read to us every night.* 3. To learn or become informed through written or printed material: *We're reading about the sun.* 4. To show by letters or numbers: *The speedometer reads 50 miles per hour.* 5. To copy information from a computer storage device, such as a disk, into memory.
read (rēd) verb read (rĕd), **reading**
* These sound alike: **read, reed**

38. Use the pronunciation key in this dictionary shown below to pronounce the word <u>read</u> as used in definition 5.

    A. păt
    B. pāy
    C. pĕt
    D. bē

ă pat	ĭ pit	oi **oil**	th bath
ā pay	ī ride	ŏŏ book	*th* bathe
â care	î fierce	ōō boot	ə ago, item
ä father	ŏ pot	ou **out**	pencil
ĕ pet	ō go	ŭ cut	atom
ē be	ô paw, for	û fur	circus

39. In which section of the library would you find a nonfiction book on Joan of Arc?
    A. biography section
    B. reference section
    C. mystery section
    D. juvenile section

40. In which section of the library would you find information on Japan?
    A. biography section
    B. reference section
    C. mystery section
    D. juvenile section

If you don't know an answer, eliminate choices that you know are wrong, and then guess.

Lesson Three: Information Skills (cont.)

Review

1. Read all charts, maps, and graphs carefully.

2. Decide what you think the answer is before reading the choices.

3. Read all choices before answering the question.

4. Choose your answer carefully. More than one choice may *seem* correct.

5. It's usually not a good idea to change your answers.

6. If you don't know an answer, eliminate choices that you know are wrong, and then guess.

Helpful Math Strategies

Test Tips

1. Use all the time that is provided. This is a test, not a race.
2. Use your time wisely.
3. Do not spend too much time on any one problem.
4. Skip hard questions and answer the easy ones first.
5. Read each problem carefully; know what you are being asked to do.
6. Read the problem twice if you have to.
7. Avoid answer sheet errors.

Math Strategies

★ Math tests usually have sections where you are asked to solve problems that test your understanding of important math concepts.

★ Be sure to check your work.

★ Recognize a reasonable answer so you can eliminate answers that don't make sense.

★ Don't get tricked; the right answer may not be given.

★ Check your work by reversing the problem.

★ Do all of your work on scratch paper.

★ Draw a picture or diagram to help you solve word problems.

★ Try the guess-and-check strategy: guess based on information in the problem, and then check it and revise it until you get the problem solved.

★ Know important math terms and vocabulary.

Name: _____ Date: _____

Unit Three: Mathematics

Lesson One: Concepts

Directions: Answer each question as indicated.

1. If a large rock equals *ten* and a small rock equals *one*, what is the total number represented here?
    A.   5
    B.   50
    C.   23
    D.   30

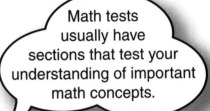

Math tests usually have sections that test your understanding of important math concepts.

2. What does the 5 in 59 stand for?
    A.   500
    B.   50
    C.   5
    D.   0

3. What place is shown by the 9 in 59?
    A.   hundreds
    B.   tens
    C.   ones
    D.   zero

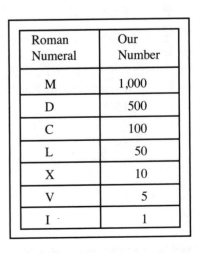

4. What number comes next in this sequence?
    A.   3,000,000
    B.   300,000
    C.   30,000
    D.   30,000,000

    30; 300; 3,000; 30,000; _____

5. Which of these is the Roman numeral for 1,163?
    A.   MXLCIII
    B.   MCXLIII
    C.   ICXIII
    D.   MCLXIII

6. In our number system, what does the Roman numeral **CCLVI** stand for?
    A.   776
    B.   256
    C.   186
    D.   56

Roman Numeral	Our Number
M	1,000
D	500
C	100
L	50
X	10
V	5
I	1

Name: _____ Date: _____

Lesson One: Concepts (cont.)

7. What are the correct numerals for the number in the box?
   A. 18,367
   B. 10,830,067
   C. 100,800,300,670
   D. 1,836

   > 1 ten thousand, 8 thousands, 3 hundreds, 6 tens, 7 ones

8. Which of these number sentences is true?
   A. $7 \neq 7$
   B. $13 \geq 15$
   C. $6 \leq 4$
   D. $4 \leq 7$

9. If I picked up 12 shells on Monday, 21 on Tuesday, 10 on Wednesday, and 14 on Thursday, how many shells would I have?
   A. 56
   B. 57
   C. 59
   D. 60

   > Do all of your work on scratch paper.

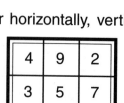

10. Which of these represents 742,521 in expanded notation?
    A. 742,000 + 521
    B. 700,000 + 40,000 + 2,000 + 500 + 20 + 1
    C. 742,521
    D. seven hundred forty-two thousand, five hundred twenty-one

11. A "magic square" is one that adds up to the same number horizontally, vertically, and diagonally. What is the "magic" number for this square?

    A. 16
    B. 18
    C. 15
    D. 12

4	9	2
3	5	7
8	1	6

12. If you round 246 to the nearest tens, the number would be
    A. 240
    B. 250
    C. 245
    D. 200

Name: _____   Date: _____

Lesson One: Concepts (cont.)

13. What number would you get when you round 7,932 to the nearest thousand?
   A. 7,000
   B. 8,000
   C. 7,900
   D. 8,932

14. Mohammed and Ali were playing a video game. Mohammed scored 428 points, and Ali scored 132. Estimate how many more points Mohammed scored than Ali.
   A. 500
   B. 300
   C. 600
   D. 560

15. What multiples are missing in this series of numbers?
   A. 20 and 36
   B. 24 and 32
   C. 24 and 36
   D. 20 and 32

   6, 12, 18, _____, 30, _____

16. What are the missing multiples in this series?
   A. 5 and 10
   B. 4 and 5
   C. 6 and 10
   D. 6 and 9

   3, _____, _____, 12, 15

17. What is the average of these numbers? 21, 34, 44
   A. 99
   B. 66
   C. 33
   D. 60

18. Jody scored 20, 15, 32, and 21 points in 4 basketball games. How many points did she average?
   A. 22
   B. $21\frac{1}{2}$
   C. 25
   D. 86

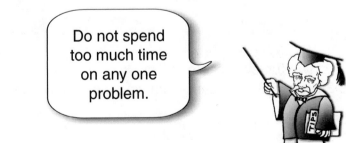

Do not spend too much time on any one problem.

Name: _____   Date: _____

Lesson One: Concepts (cont.)

19. If you wanted to measure the length of your desk, which of these measurement tools would you use?
    A. ruler
    B. yardstick
    C. stopwatch
    D. thermometer

20. If you wanted to measure the time it takes your mom to run 3 miles, which tool would you use?
    A. ruler
    B. yardstick
    C. stopwatch
    D. thermometer

Read each problem <u>very</u> carefully.

21. It took Barbara 4 days and 6 hours to sell her Girl Scout Cookies. It took her sister Carol 3 days and 10 hours to sell hers. How much time did the girls spend altogether selling cookies?
    A. 7 days and 16 hours
    B. 8 days and 4 hours
    C. 8 days and 2 hours
    D. 7 days and 4 hours

22. Matt carried a bag with 3 pounds and 6 ounces of potatoes and 2 pounds and 5 ounces of onions for his mother. How heavy was his bag?
    A. 5 lbs., 11 oz.
    B. 1 lb., 1 oz.
    C. 6 lbs., 2 oz.
    D. none of these

23. Mrs. Readen needs to triple her recipe that calls for 1 pint, 2 ounces of milk. How much milk does she need?
    A. 1 qt., 6 oz.
    B. 2 qts., 2 oz.
    C. 3 pts., 6 oz.
    D. 4 pts., 6 oz.

24. Mrs. Jackson cooked two turkey breasts at Thanksgiving. One was 4 pounds, 8 ounces, and the other was 3 pounds, 12 ounces. What was the total weight of her turkeys?
    A. 7 lbs., 15 oz.
    B. 7 lbs., 16 oz.
    C. 8 lbs., 20 oz.
    D. 8 lbs., 4 oz.

Name: _____ Date: _____

Lesson One: Concepts (cont.)

25. If 2 lb., 4 oz. of candy are divided among 3 boys, how much does each boy receive?
    A.   12 oz.
    B.   3 lbs.
    C.   12 lbs.
    D.   36 oz.

26. How many seconds are there in one hour?

    A.   60 seconds
    B.   76,400 seconds
    C.   3,600 seconds
    D.   none of these

27. Examine the Weebles and the non-Weebles. Which of these is a Weeble?

    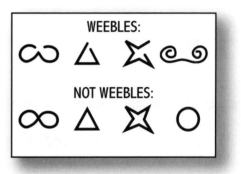

    A.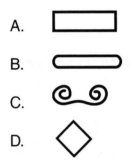

    B.

    C.

    D.

28. Using this spinner, what is the probability of spinning a 4?

    A.   1 : 4
    B.   1 : 8
    C.   2 : 6
    D.   3 : 8

29. Katie went shopping and bought 3 pairs of jeans and 3 shirts. If every shirt went with every pair of jeans, how many different outfits can she make?

    A.   9
    B.   6
    C.   12
    D.   None of these

Name: _____   Date: _____

Lesson One: Concepts (cont.)

30. Which of these people was a famous mathematician?

  A. Caesar
  B. Euclid
  C. Madonna
  D. Newton

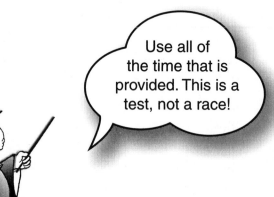

Use all of the time that is provided. This is a test, not a race!

Review

1. Math tests usually have sections that test your understanding of important math concepts.

2. Do not spend too much time on any one problem.

3. Do all of your work on scratch paper.

4. Read each problem carefully.

5. Use all of the time that is provided. This is a test, not a race!

Name: _____ Date: _____

Unit Three: Mathematics

Lesson Two: Computation

Directions: Solve the following problems as directed.

1. 123 + 12 + 210 + 24 =

    A. 460
    B. 369
    C. 693
    D. none of these

2. 35,432 + 23,517 =

    A. 68,949
    B. 59,949
    C. 58,949
    D. 48,949

3. What is the sum of 73 feet, 69 feet, and 91 feet?

    A. 232 feet
    B. 333 feet
    C. 235 feet
    D. none of these

4. How much less is 212 than 632?

    A. 844
    B. 400
    C. 240
    D. 420

5. 8,543 - 2,123 =

    A. 6,230
    B. 6,420
    C. 8,666
    D. none of these

Name: _____ Date: _____

Lesson Two: Computation (cont.)

6.   Subtract $3.74 from $5.00.

     A. $1.26
     B. $8.74
     C. $2.74
     D.   none of these

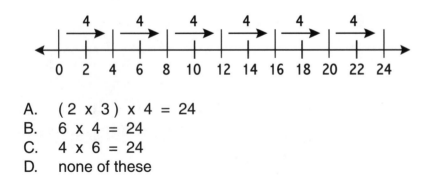

Do the problem first. Then compare with the given choices.

7.   3,814 - 1,859 =

     A.   5,672
     B.   1,955
     C.   4,065
     D.   2,045

8.   463
      - 209

     A.   254
     B.   672
     C.   266
     D.   none of these

9.   63 x 4 =

     A.   242
     B.   422
     C.   252
     D.   272

10.   694
      x 38

     A.   5,632
     B.   26,372
     C.   732
     D.   none of these

11.   Choose the equation that is represented on the number line.

    0   2   4   6   8   10   12   14   16   18   20   22   24

     A.   (2 x 3) x 4 = 24
     B.   6 x 4 = 24
     C.   4 x 6 = 24
     D.   none of these

Name: _____ Date: _____

Lesson Two: Computation (cont.)

12. 124 x 100 =
    A.   12,400
    B.   124
    C.   124,000
    D.   1,240

13. What is the area of this sheet of drawing paper? ($a = l \times w$)

    A.   32 square inches
    B.   108 square inches
    C.   225 square inches
    D.   252 square inches

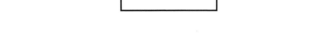

18"
14"

14. What is the perimeter of a square whose sides measure 6 inches? ($P = 2l + 2w$)

    A.   72 inches
    B.   24 inches
    C.   144 inches
    D.   none of these

6"

15. 487 x 89 =

    A.   576
    B.   43,343
    C.   4,334
    D.   none of these

16.   54,260
   x   23

    A.   162,780
    B.   1,085,200
    C.   1,247,980
    D.   10,085,200

17. 4)208‾

    A.   54
    B.   52
    C.   12
    D.   none of these

Don't be tricked. The right answer may not be given.

Name: _____ Date: _____

Lesson Two: Computation (cont.)

18. $513 \div 3 =$

    A.   176   C.   171

    B.   52   D.   none of these

19. $3\overline{)\$312}$

    A. $104   C. $371

    B. $10   D.   none of these

20. Which of these fractions is the largest?

    A. $\frac{2}{3}$ C. $\frac{1}{2}$

    B. $\frac{5}{12}$ D. $\frac{1}{6}$

21. What is the simplest form of the fraction $\frac{12}{32}$?

    A. $\frac{1}{4}$ C. $\frac{3}{8}$

    B. $\frac{4}{14}$ D. none of these

22. In our class, there are 27 students, 17 of which are boys. What fraction of our class is boys?

    A. $\frac{10}{27}$ C. $\frac{27}{17}$

    B. $\frac{17}{27}$ D. $\frac{6}{9}$

23. What fraction of this circle is shaded?

    A. $\frac{1}{3}$ C. $\frac{1}{8}$

    B. $\frac{1}{2}$ D. $\frac{1}{4}$

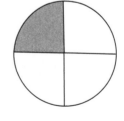

24. $\frac{5}{8} + \frac{1}{4} =$

    A. $\frac{7}{8}$ C. $\frac{1}{8}$

    B. $\frac{6}{12}$ D. none of these

Name: _____ Date: _____

Lesson Two: Computation (cont.)

25. $7\frac{3}{8}$ - $4\frac{1}{4}$ =

    A. $5\frac{3}{8}$ C. $3\frac{5}{8}$

    B. $11\frac{2}{3}$ D. none of these

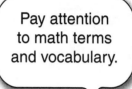

Pay attention to math terms and vocabulary.

26.   106.935
     - 95.824

    A. 111.1   C. 11.111
    B. 111.11   D. none of these

27. 36.3 + 50.10 =

    A. 86.04   C. 53.73
    B. 43.61   D. 86.4

28. Which of the numbers below is the least common multiple of 6 and 8?

    A. 6   C. 24
    B. 14   D. 8

29. $6\frac{1}{2}$ - $3\frac{3}{4}$ =

    A. $1\frac{1}{2}$ C. $5\frac{1}{4}$

    B. $3\frac{3}{4}$ D. $2\frac{3}{4}$

30. Which two lines intersect?

    A. AC, BD
    B. AB, CD
    C. EF, GH
    D. DE, FG

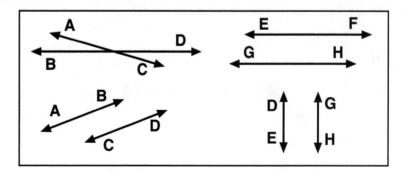

Name: _____ Date: _____

Lesson Two: Computation (cont.)

31. Which figure is symmetrical?

A.　　　B.　　　C.　　　D.

32. Which of these shows a line of symmetry?

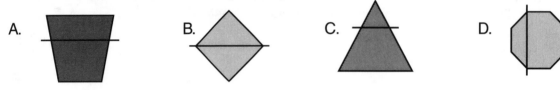

A.　　　B.　　　C.　　　D.

33. Which of these shows a pair of congruent figures?

A.　　　B.　　　C.　　　D.

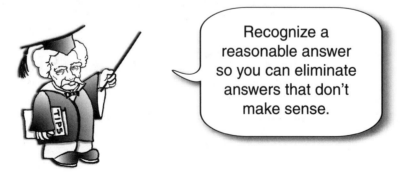

Recognize a reasonable answer so you can eliminate answers that don't make sense.

Name: _____ Date: _____

Lesson Two: Computation (cont.)

34. What is the diameter of this circle?

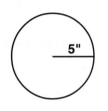

    A.   10 inches
    B.   12 inches
    C.   16 inches
    D.   none of these

35. Which has more volume?

    A.   a quart bottle of soda
    B.   a balloon that holds two pints of water
    C.   a mixing bowl that can hold eight cups
    D.   a gallon of milk

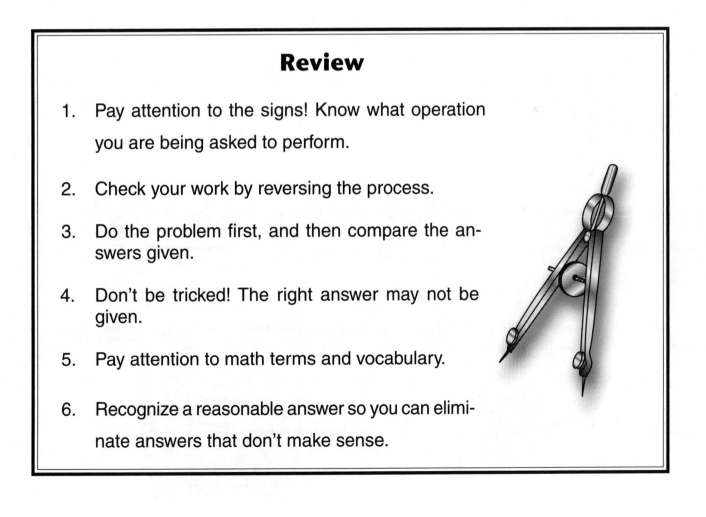

Review

1. Pay attention to the signs! Know what operation you are being asked to perform.

2. Check your work by reversing the process.

3. Do the problem first, and then compare the answers given.

4. Don't be tricked! The right answer may not be given.

5. Pay attention to math terms and vocabulary.

6. Recognize a reasonable answer so you can eliminate answers that don't make sense.

Name: _____   Date: _____

UNIT THREE: MATHEMATICS

Lesson Three: Problem Solving and Reasoning

Directions: Answer each question as indicated.

1. A newspaper cost 50¢ before the price was increased by 35¢. What is its present cost?
    A.   85¢
    B.   75¢
    C.   90¢
    D.   none of these

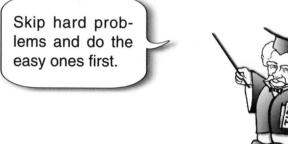

Skip hard problems and do the easy ones first.

2. Yesterday I had 63¢ more than I have today. Today I have $1.12. How much did I have yesterday?
    A. $1.52
    B. $1.75
    C. $0.49
    D. $1.51

3. Paul collects Pepsi™ cans. This month, he added 24 to the 568 he already has. How many cans does Paul have?
    A.   492
    B.   600
    C.   592
    D.   544

4. How many more cans does he need to reach 600 cans?
    A.   8
    B.   7
    C.   10
    D.   4

5. A man weighed 218 pounds before he went on a diet. He lost 39 pounds on this diet. How much does he weigh now?
    A.   240 lbs.
    B.   257 lbs.
    C.   50 lbs.
    D.   179 lbs.

Name: _____ Date: _____

Lesson Three: Problem Solving and Reasoning (cont.)

6. Sarah bought a special sweater for $38 and gave the cashier $50. How much change will Sarah get?
   A. $1.25
   B. 12¢
   C. $12
   D. none of these

> Try drawing a picture or diagram on scratch paper to help you solve the problem.

7. At the orchard, workers picked 378 baskets of apples a day. Each basket holds 65 apples. How many apples are picked every day?
   A. 313
   B. 443
   C. 24,570
   D. none of these

8. Using the chart below, what is the cost of 4 pounds of chicken breasts and 2 pounds of chicken legs?

   A. $7.20
   B. $1.98
   C. $9.18
   D. none of these

Mom's Meat Market	
Chicken breasts	$1.80 lb.
Chicken legs	$0.99 lb.

9. Our family of 5 went to a movie on Friday. The cost of admission was $8 per person. What was the total cost of admission for our family?
   A. $13
   B. $35
   C. $40
   D. $45

10. Zoe's dad won $519 in a drawing and wanted to divide it equally among his three children. How much did each child receive?
    A. $171
    B. $173
    C. $371
    D. none of these

> Use the "guess-and-check" strategy: guess the answer from the information given, and try the problem. If you are wrong, try another answer until you successfully solve the problem.

Name: _____ Date: _____

Lesson Three: Problem Solving and Reasoning (cont.)

11. Using the calendar at the right, what is the date of the third Monday in the month?
    A. 3
    B. 10
    C. 17
    D. 24

12. How many Saturdays are in the month?
    A. 4
    B. 5
    C. 6
    D. none of these

13. What is the last day of the month?
    A. Sunday
    B. Monday
    C. Tuesday
    D. Saturday

MARCH						
Sun.	Mon.	Tues.	Wed.	Thurs.	Fri.	Sat.
						1
2	3	4	5	6	7	8
9	10	11	12	13	14	15
16	17	18	19	20	21	22
23	24	25	26	27	28	29
30	31					

14. Marsha has a dental appointment two weeks from March 21st. What will the date of her appointment be?
    A. 28th
    B. 7th
    C. 4th
    D. not enough information

15. Using the figure at the right, who lives at B,6?
    A. Mike
    B. Anne
    C. Mary
    D. Miguel

16. What is the location of Chloe's house?
    A. E,7
    B. F,7
    C. E,6
    D. D,7

17. Whose house is the only one on line 2?
    A. Miguel
    B. Grace
    C. Toni
    D. Andre

Name: _____   Date: _____

Lesson Three: Problem Solving and Reasoning (cont.)

18. What time will it be 35 minutes after the time shown on this digital clock?
    A. 6:80
    B. 7:20
    C. 7:00
    D. not enough information

19. What time is it $4\frac{1}{2}$ hours after 10:00 A.M.?
    A. 1:30
    B. 2:00
    C. 2:30
    D. 3:00

20. Tammy goes to school every day from 7:30 to 3:30. Then she goes to soccer practice for $1\frac{1}{2}$ hours and ballet lessons for 1 hour. What time does she finally get home each day?
    A. 6:00   C. 6:30
    B. 4:30   D. not enough information given

21. What comes next in this pattern?

    A. □
    B. ○
    C. ▯
    D. ◁

22. What number is missing in this triangle pattern?
    A. 48
    B. 28
    C. 44
    D. 23

```
          1
        2   3
      3   5   8
    4   7  12  20
  5   9  16  28   ?
```

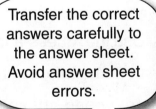

Transfer the correct answers carefully to the answer sheet. Avoid answer sheet errors.

23. The train for Springfield leaves Jake's Junction at 8:30 A.M. and arrives at 10:15 A.M. How long is the trip?
    A. 1 hour, 30 minutes
    B. 1 hour, 15 minutes
    C. 1 hour, 45 minutes
    D. 2 hours

Name: _____ Date: _____

Lesson Three: Problem Solving and Reasoning (cont.)

24. The Fallali family drove their camper on a three-day trip. The first day they drove 6 hours, 10 minutes. The second day they drove 5 hours, 30 minutes. The last day they drove 5 hours, 40 minutes. How long did they travel in all?
    A.   16 hours, 20 minutes
    B.   17 hours, 20 minutes
    C.   17 hours
    D.   16 hours, 40 minutes

25. The children in the Johnson family are 13, 10, 8, 5, 3, and 3. What is the average age of these children?
    A.   6
    B.   3
    C.   7
    D.   42

Review

1. Skip hard problems and do the easy ones first.

2. Try drawing a picture or a diagram on scratch paper to help you solve the problem.

3. Use the "guess-and-check" strategy: guess the answer from the information given and try the problem. If you are wrong, try another answer until you successfully solve the problem.

4. Transfer the correct answers carefully to the answer sheet. Avoid answer sheet errors.

Helpful Science Strategies

Test Tips

1. Work as quickly as you can.
2. Skip the hard questions and answer the easy ones first; go back to the hard questions when you finish.
3. Use common sense when looking at your answer choices.
4. Answer all questions.
5. Think twice before changing an answer; your first guess is usually the correct one.
6. When all else fails, guess!
7. If you change an answer, be sure to erase your pencil marks completely.
8. Often information in a later question can be used to answer an earlier question.
9. Pay attention to key words like *not, but, except, always, never,* and *only*.

Science Strategies

★ Science test questions usually cover information about life science, physical science, earth science, and health science.

★ Pay close attention to how the questions are worded. All answers may be *true*, but only one answers the question.

★ Keep in mind the steps of the scientific process.

★ Use logical reasoning to answer the questions. Does your answer make sense?

★ Use the process of elimination to find answers. Cross out those that you *know* are wrong.

★ Examine charts, pictures, diagrams, and figures carefully.

Name: _____   Date: _____

UNIT FOUR: SCIENCE

Lesson One: Process and Inquiry

Directions: Choose the best answer for each question.

1. Which one of these is something scientists do?
   A. They have all the answers.
   B. They make rules about nature.
   C. They write textbooks.
   D. They ask a lot of questions.

Keep in mind the steps of the scientific process.

2. All of these are steps in an experiment except
   A. asking a question.
   B. looking in a book for the answer.
   C. recording data.
   D. drawing conclusions.

Directions: Use the chart in Figure 1 to answer questions 3–5.

3. Birds taking baths in birdbaths is an example of
   A. migration.
   B. a learned behavior.
   C. instinct.
   D. hibernation.

4. All of these are examples of instinctive behavior except
   A. bears hibernating.
   B. whales storing extra fat.
   C. birds sitting on nests.
   D. seals playing with a ball.

BIRD BEHAVIOR	
Learned	**Instinct**
• **what to eat** • **how to fly**	• **nest building** • **migrating south**

Figure 1

5. What conclusion can you draw from the data in Figure 1?
   A. A behavior that an animal is born with is a learned behavior.
   B. A behavior that an animal is born with is instinctive behavior.
   C. A behavior that an animal learns is a demonstrated behavior.
   D. A behavior that an animal is born with is a demonstrated behavior.

Name: _____ Date: _____

Lesson One: Process and Inquiry (cont.)

6. Scientists search for new information through which one of these?
    A. experimenting
    B. migrating
    C. hibernating
    D. writing

7. All but which one of these is important when experimenting?
    A. following directions
    B. communicating with others
    C. taking accurate notes
    D. finding the right answers

Pay close attention to how the questions are worded.

8. Forming a *hypothesis* means
    A. making an educated guess as to what will happen in an experiment.
    B. developing a relationship between scientist and nature.
    C. developing complex classifications of plants and animals.
    D. identifying and testing variables.

9. All of these are part of the scientific method except
    A. observing.
    B. predicting.
    C. learning.
    D. recording.

Directions: Use the chart in Figure 2 to answer questions 10–12.

10. Between which two grades do students grow the most?
    A. 1 and 2
    B. 2 and 3
    C. 4 and 5
    D. 5 and 6

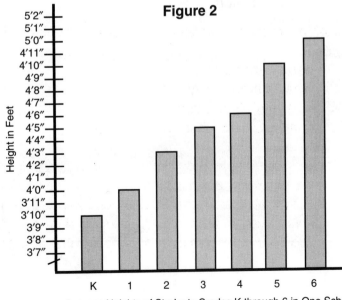

Figure 2

Average Heights of Students Grades K through 6 in One School

Name: _____ Date: _____

Lesson One: Process and Inquiry (cont.)

11. The smallest difference in height is between grades
    A. 2–3.
    B. 3–4.
    C. 5–6.
    D. 1–2.

Work as quickly as you can.

12. What is the difference in height between K and 6?
    A. 2'
    B. 1'4"
    C. 1'2"
    D. 2'2"

13. Which one of these is a scientific fact?
    A. Dinosaurs ruled the earth.
    B. Dinosaurs could neither swim nor fly.
    C. Dinosaurs were awesome.
    D. Dinosaurs became extinct.

14. Which one of these is an opinion?
    A. Scientists have identified over 500 types of dinosaurs.
    B. The word *dinosaur* means "terrible lizard."
    C. Dinosaurs became extinct because the earth became too hot.
    D. Brontosauruses weighed up to 30 tons.

15. "Dinosaurs evolved into many different species," is an example of a scientific
    A. fact.
    B. opinion.
    C. generalization.
    D. theory.

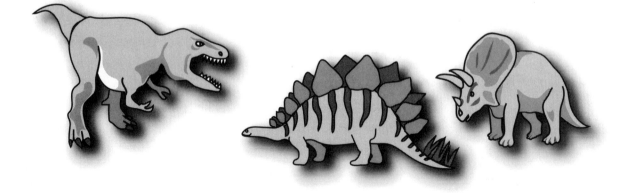

Name: _____ Date: _____

Lesson One: Process and Inquiry (cont.)

Directions: Use the information in Figure 3 to answer questions 16–18.

Series Circuit

Parallel Circuit

Figure 3

16. When you screw in the bulbs in the circuits in the drawing, what will happen?
    A. The series circuit will burn less brightly than the parallel circuit.
    B. The parallel circuit will burn less brightly than the series circuit.
    C. The bulbs in the series circuit will burn out.
    D. The bulbs in the parallel circuit will burn out.

17. Predict what would happen in the series circuit if just one of the lights burns out.
    A. The first one will burn out the second one.
    B. The other one will not light.
    C. The other one will stay lit.
    D. The circuit will get very hot.

18. Predict what would happen in a parallel circuit if just one of the lights burns out.
    A. The other one will not light.
    B. The other one will stay lit.
    C. The first one will burn out the second one.
    D. The circuit will get very hot.

Think twice before changing an answer.

Name: _____ Date: _____

Lesson One: Process and Inquiry (cont.)

19. Which of these conclusions could you make from data given in Figure 4?
    A. Materials made from wood are good conductors.
    B. Materials made of metal are good conductors.
    C. Materials made from paper are good conductors.
    D. Materials made from rubber are good conductors.

20. Using the information in Figure 4, which prediction could you make?
    A. A sugar cube would be a good conductor.
    B. A coin would be a good conductor.
    C. Water would be a good conductor.
    D. A tire would be a good conductor.

21. Which conclusion could you make from Figure 5 below?
    A. Don't touch the sail.
    B. Don't touch the sides of the boat.
    C. Don't touch the center pole.
    D. Don't touch the ropes.

Item Tested		Conductor	Insulator
Aluminum Foil		✔	
Door Key		✔	
Paper Cup			✔
Coin		✔	
Pencil			✔
Rubber Band			✔
Ruler			✔

Figure 4

Answer all questions, even if you have to guess.

Figure 5

Name: _____ Date: _____

Lesson One: Process and Inquiry (cont.)

22. In Figure 6, what does the globe represent?
    A. North Pole
    B. Earth
    C. daylight
    D. land

23. In Figure 6, what does the flashlight represent?
    A. the sun
    B. the moon
    C. stars
    D. another planet

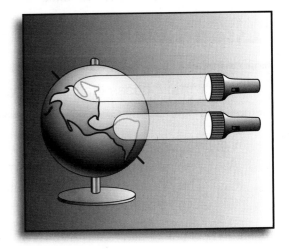

Figure 6

24. Which statement is true?
    A. The equator receives indirect rays from the sun.
    B. The Poles receive direct rays from the sun.
    C. The Poles receive indirect rays from the sun.
    D. Indirect rays of sun are better than direct rays from the sun.

25. All of these behaviors indicate a positive attitude toward science except
    A. using extra time for science investigations.
    B. finding out what careers there are in science.
    C. getting a stomachache on the day you have a science test.
    D. volunteering to care for classroom pets.

Review

1. Keep in mind the steps of the scientific process.

2. Pay close attention to how the questions are worded.

3. Work as quickly as you can.

4. Think twice before changing an answer.

5. Answer all questions even if you have to guess.

Name: _____ Date: _____

UNIT FOUR: SCIENCE

Lesson Two: Concepts

Directions: Choose the best answer for each question.

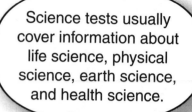

Science tests usually cover information about life science, physical science, earth science, and health science.

1. Why do the leaves on plants grow toward the light?
   A. They don't really; it just seems as if they do.
   B. They need the bugs in the air for food.
   C. They use the sunlight to make food.
   D. Gravity forces them toward the light.

2. Which of these is the term for this process?
   A. phototropism
   B. thermotropism
   C. hydrotropism
   D. chemotropism

3. How does losing leaves in the fall help some trees survive?
   A. Trees keep from losing water they can't replace.
   B. Trees can't get the water they need to grow.
   C. Trees can protect their branches from the cold of winter.
   D. Trees get more sunlight this way.

4. What part of the plant is labeled *4* in Figure 1?
   A. root
   B. stem
   C. leaves
   D. flower

5. Of what importance is the part of the plant labeled *1* in Figure 1?
   A. It carries water and minerals away from the leaves.
   B. It contains the seeds to make a new plant.
   C. It anchors the plant to the earth.
   D. It holds the leaves and flowers.

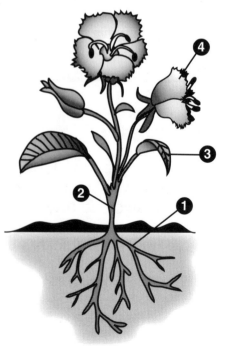

Figure 1

Name: _____   Date: _____

Lesson Two: Concepts (cont.)

6. Which one of the items in Figure 2 is a non-living thing?
    A. butterfly
    B. rock
    C. kitten
    D. tree

Figure 2

7. How are animals different from plants?
    A. Plants are multicolored; animals are not.
    B. Plants make their own food; animals don't.
    C. Animals move to face the sun, and plants don't.
    D. Animals are made of many cells, and plants are single-celled.

8. Which of these represents an accurate food chain?
    A. grasshopper → snake → hawk → frog
    B. frog → hawk → snake → grasshopper
    C. hawk → snake → frog → grasshopper
    D. hawk → frog → snake → grasshopper

9. Living things that eat other animals are called
    A. herbivores.
    B. omnivores.
    C. carnivores.
    D. hungry.

10. Animals need all but which of these to live?
    A. food
    B. shelter
    C. clothing
    D. oxygen

11. The place where an animal lives is called its
    A. habitat.
    B. environment.
    C. house.
    D. pad.

Skip the hard questions, and answer the easy ones first. Then go back and try the hard ones.

73

Name: _____   Date: _____

Lesson Two: Concepts (cont.)

Figure 3

12. Elephants, giraffes, and tigers live in which habitat in Figure 3?
    A.   grasslands
    B.   mountains
    C.   near water
    D.   desert

13. Coyotes, scorpions, and rattlesnakes live in which kind of habitat?
    A.   grasslands
    B.   mountains
    C.   near water
    D.   desert

14. Animals and plants can become endangered and possibly extinct for all these reasons except
    A.   extreme changes in climate.
    B.   destruction of their habitat.
    C.   global warming.
    D.   over-hunting.

15. Every object takes up space and has
    A.   matter.
    B.   mass.
    C.   measurement.
    D.   magic.

16. Everything we see and use is made up of basic ingredients called
    A.   matter.   C.   measurement.
    B.   mass.   D.   magic.

Use common sense when selecting your answer.

Lesson Two: Concepts (cont.)

17. Using the chart in Figure 4, how much would you weigh on Jupiter if you weighed 100 pounds on Earth?
    A. 180 pounds
    B. 118 pounds
    C. 234 pounds
    D. 117 pounds

18. On which planets would you weigh the least?
    A. Mercury and Venus
    B. Venus and Mars
    C. Mercury and Mars
    D. Venus and Jupiter

19. About how long does it take the Earth to revolve around the sun?
    A. 365 days
    B. 3,650 days
    C. 36,500 days
    D. 65 days

20. If you are ten years old, about how many days has the Earth rotated around the sun?
    A. 365 days
    B. 3,650 days
    C. 36,500 days
    D. 65 days

21. The rocky planets include all of these except
    A. Venus.
    B. Earth.
    C. Jupiter.
    D. Mars.

22. Which of these planets is *not* a frozen planet?
    A. Saturn
    B. Pluto
    C. Venus
    D. Neptune

Weight on Other Planets	
Planet	**Weight (in pounds) of 100-lb. object on Earth**
Mercury	37
Venus	88
Earth	100
Mars	37
Jupiter	234
Saturn	115
Uranus	117
Neptune	118

Figure 4

Often information in a later question can be used to answer an earlier question.

Name: _____ Date: _____

Lesson Two: Concepts (cont.)

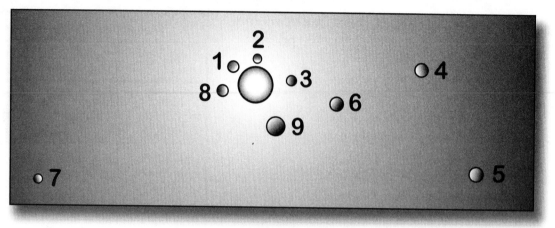

Figure 5

23. Figure 5 represents our solar system. Which planet is number 5?
    A. Venus
    B. Saturn
    C. Neptune
    D. Pluto

24. Pluto is which planet in Figure 5?
    A. 9
    B. 8
    C. 7
    D. 6

25. Your skeleton does all but which one of these?
    A. It supports your body parts.
    B. It forms your muscles.
    C. It protects your organs.
    D. It gives shape to your body.

26. Exercise gives you all but which one of these?
    A. strength
    B. flexibility
    C. endurance
    D. courage

27. Proper food, sleep, and rest are important for
    A. bodybuilding.
    B. physical fitness.
    C. weight loss.
    D. marathon running.

> If you change your answer, be sure to erase your pencil mark completely.

Lesson Two: Concepts (cont.)

28. The earth is surrounded by a thin blanket of gases called the
   A.   stratosphere.
   B.   thermosphere.
   C.   atmosphere.
   D.   clouds.

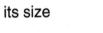

29. A drought is a serious situation because
   A.   flooding could occur.
   B.   living things need water to live.
   C.   it leads to global warming.
   D.   some people die in hot weather.

30. What causes thunder?
   A.   rain clouds
   B.   the aurora
   C.   lightning
   D.   a sonic boom

31. Which one of these is not true?
   A.   Cirrus clouds are thin, feather-like clouds in patches or narrow bands.
   B.   Cumulus clouds are dark, ominous clouds.
   C.   Clouds come from moisture in the air.
   D.   High clouds are composed mostly of ice crystals.

32. Weather is the result of which one of these?
   A.   the water cycle
   B.   air masses
   C.   interactions among air, water, earth, and heat from the sun
   D.   long bands of winds moving rapidly from west to east

33. What determines if an object will float in water?
   A.   its mass   B.   its weight   C.   its size   D.   its density

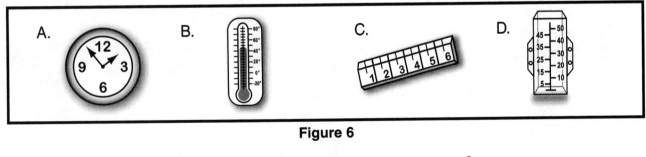

Figure 6

34. Which of the objects in Figure 6 above measures temperature?
   A.   D   B.   C   C.   B   D.   A

Name: _____ Date: _____

Lesson Two: Concepts (cont.)

35. Look at Figure 7. Why does the balloon in the warm Coke™ bottle inflate and the one in the cold Coke™ bottle doesn't?
    A.   because cool air takes up less space
    B.   because cool air takes up more space
    C.   because warm air rises
    D.   because the air in the warm bottle cooled

36. Which is an example of mechanical energy?
    A.   a lamp
    B.   a VCR
    C.   a power plant
    D.   a boy raking leaves

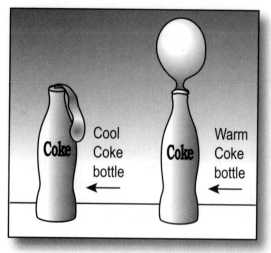

Figure 7

37. What are fiber optics?
    A.   rods of glass, thinner than a hair, that carry information as coded flashes of laser light
    B.   low power of radio waves that flow through the air
    C.   wires that carry television and radio waves to computers
    D.   very thin telephone wires buried underground

38. What is DNA?
    A.   a molecule that contains all the information about that organism
    B.   tiny pieces of a secret code that does not attract other organisms
    C.   a tiny structure made of protoplasm containing organelles
    D.   the place that contains an organism's enzymes

39. All but which one of these is a famous scientist?
    A.   Charles Darwin
    B.   Marie Curie
    C.   Louis Pasteur
    D.   Pedro Martinez

40. Which of these does not represent a career in science?
    A.   zoologist
    B.   geologist
    C.   theologist
    D.   volcanologist

When all else fails, guess!

Name: _____ Date: _____

Lesson Two: Concepts (cont.)

Review

1. Science tests usually cover information about life science, physical science, earth science, and health science.

2. Skip the hard questions, and answer the easy ones first. Then go back and try the hard ones.

3. Use common sense when selecting your answer.

4. Often information in a later question can be used to answer an earlier question.

5. If you change an answer, be sure to erase your pencil mark completely.

6. When all else fails, guess!

Helpful Social Studies Strategies

Test Tips

1. Control your test anxiety. Take deep, deep breaths to calm your nervous energy; however, a little nervous energy sharpens the brain.
2. Don't panic; you are not supposed to know *everything* on the test.
3. Stay calm and focused. Don't let your mind wander.
4. Read and consider all answer choices; there may be a better answer farther down the list, so don't be too anxious.

Social Studies Strategies

★ Social studies is about people, places, and events and when and how they happened.

★ Social studies tests usually include questions about maps, geography, history, and government.

★ When you read a map, be sure to read the title first. Make sure you understand the kind of information the map is giving.

★ When presented with a passage to read about a social studies topic, read the questions *before* you read the passage so you know what to look for.

★ For multiple choice questions, eliminate unreasonable answers first. Then choose.

★ When you don't know the answer, take your best guess.

★ Read maps, graphs, tables, and data charts very carefully.

Name: _____ Date: _____

UNIT FIVE: SOCIAL STUDIES

Lesson One: History and Culture

Directions: Study the time line, "Voyages of Discovery," and then answer questions 1–5.

Voyages of Discovery

Bartolomeu Dias discovers the Cape of Good Hope.	Christopher Columbus discovers the islands of San Salvador, Cuba, and Hispaniola.	John Cabot discovers Newfoundland and the North American continent.	Vasco da Gama discovers a trade route to India.	Magellan discovers the Philippine Islands.	Jacques Cartier discovers the mainland of Canada.	Henry Hudson discovers Hudson Bay.
1488	1492	1497	1498	1512	1535	1610

1. According to the time line, which continent was discovered first?
   A. South America
   B. North America
   C. Canada
   D. Africa

2. What country did Columbus think he discovered?
   A. Mexico
   B. Canada
   C. Japan
   D. India

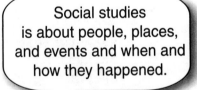

Social studies is about people, places, and events and when and how they happened.

3. What country did he actually discover?
   A. Mexico
   B. San Salvador
   C. Brazil
   D. India

Name: _____ Date: _____

Lesson One: History and Culture (cont.)

4. Which explorer discovered North America?
    A. Ferdinand Magellan
    B. John Cabot
    C. Jacques Cartier
    D. Henry Hudson

5. This explorer was not able to find a passage to India, but his important explorations led the way to many valuable and important discoveries.
    A. Ferdinand Magellan
    B. John Cabot
    C. Jacques Cartier
    D. Henry Hudson

6. What area did Lewis and Clark explore?
    A. Island of Manhattan
    B. Louisiana Purchase
    C. the Great Plains
    D. Oregon Trail

7. Why do Americans pledge allegiance to the American flag?
    A. because it is a symbol of the United States
    B. because it is the right thing to do
    C. because we are loyal citizens
    D. because you will go to jail if you don't

Eliminate unreasonable answers first, and then make your choice!

8. Which of these American monuments is *not* located in Washington, D.C.?
    A. the Jefferson Memorial
    B. the Lincoln Memorial
    C. the Washington Monument
    D. the Crazy Horse Memorial

9. A gift from France, this famous lady greets all visitors to New York City:
    A. the Great Pyramid
    B. the Sphinx
    C. the Statue of Liberty
    D. the Taj Majal

10. The last star was added to our flag in 1959 for the state of:
    A. Alaska
    B. Hawaii
    C. Haiti
    D. Cuba

Name: _____ Date: _____

Lesson One: History and Culture (cont.)

11. Which of these signs signals a pedestrian crossing?

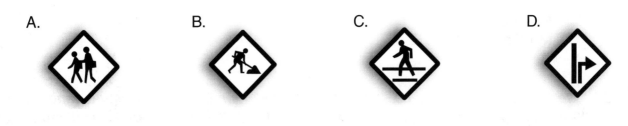

A.   B.   C.   D.

Directions: Use the graph "Religious Membership in the United States" to answer questions 12–14.

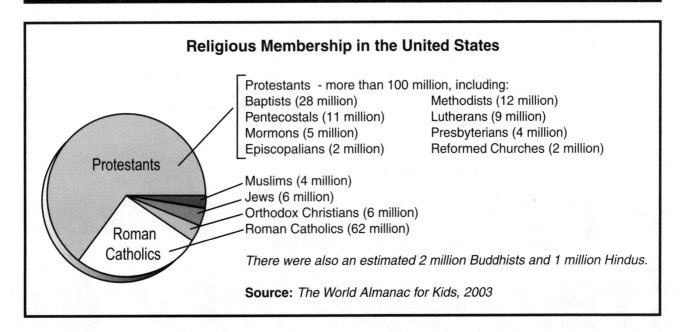

Religious Membership in the United States

Protestants - more than 100 million, including:
Baptists (28 million)   Methodists (12 million)
Pentecostals (11 million)   Lutherans (9 million)
Mormons (5 million)   Presbyterians (4 million)
Episcopalians (2 million)   Reformed Churches (2 million)

Muslims (4 million)
Jews (6 million)
Orthodox Christians (6 million)
Roman Catholics (62 million)

Protestants

Roman Catholics

There were also an estimated 2 million Buddhists and 1 million Hindus.

Source: *The World Almanac for Kids, 2003*

12. What is the largest religious group in the United States?
    A.   Protestants
    B.   Catholics
    C.   Muslims
    D.   Jews

> Read maps, graphs, tables, and charts very carefully.

13. There are about the same number of Muslims as there are
    A.   Mormons.
    B.   Baptists.
    C.   Presbyterians.
    D.   Methodists.

Name: _____ Date: _____

Lesson One: History and Culture (cont.)

14. More Americans are Lutheran than are
    A. Baptists.
    B. Methodists.
    C. Mormons.
    D. Roman Catholics.

15. *"We hold these truths to be self-evident, that all men are created equal, [and that they have the rights to] life, liberty and the pursuit of happiness,"* are famous words from the
    A. Articles of Confederation.
    B. United States Constitution.
    C. Declaration of Independence.
    D. Bill of Rights.

16. "The Trail of Tears" was the
    A. last major battle between Indians and U.S. troops.
    B. move of the U.S. capital from Philadelphia to Washington, D.C.
    C. forced march of the Cherokee Indians from Georgia to Oklahoma.
    D. fight for independence from Mexico by the Texans at the Alamo.

17. Who was Benedict Arnold?
    A. a general during the Mexican War
    B. a politician during the Civil War
    C. a traitor during the Revolutionary War
    D. a soldier during the Korean War

18. Which of these was *not* one of the original 13 colonies?
    A. North Carolina
    B. New York
    C. Florida
    D. Virginia

19. Which one of these people was the first person to walk on the moon?
    A. Astronaut Neil Armstrong
    B. Astronaut Sally Ride
    C. Astronaut John Glenn
    D. Actor Tom Hanks

20. Who was the first African-American on the United States Supreme Court?
    A. Condoleezza Rice
    B. General Colin Powell
    C. Martin Luther King, Jr.
    D. Thurgood Marshall

Name: _____ Date: _____

Lesson One: History and Culture (cont.)

21. Who was the first woman on the United States Supreme Court?
    A. Condoleezza Rice
    B. Oprah Winfrey
    C. Sandra Day O'Conner
    D. Ruth Bader Ginsburg

22. What significant historical event happened on December 7, 1941?
    A. Japan attacked the United States at Pearl Harbor.
    B. The United States defeated Iraq in the Persian Gulf.
    C. The federal building in Oklahoma was bombed.
    D. Hijacked jets crashed into the World Trade Center and the Pentagon.

23. What significant historical event happened on September 11, 2001?
    A. Japan attacked the United States at Pearl Harbor.
    B. The United States defeated Iraq in the Persian Gulf.
    C. The federal building in Oklahoma was bombed.
    D. Hijacked jets crashed into the World Trade Center and the Pentagon.

24. Who was called Johnny Appleseed?
    A. John Brown
    B. John Chapman
    C. John Glenn
    D. John Smith

Directions: Use the "Population" and "Area" graphs for questions 25–26.

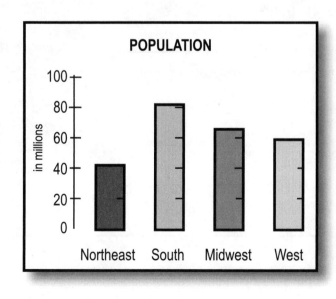

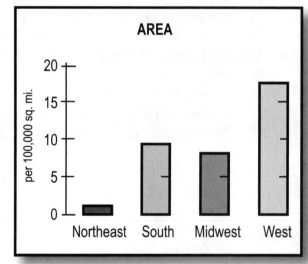

Name: _____ Date: _____

Lesson One: History and Culture (cont.)

25. Which region of the United States has the most people?
    A.   Northeast
    B.   South
    C.   Midwest
    D.   West

26. What is the largest region in the United States?
    A.   Northeast
    B.   South
    C.   Midwest
    D.   West

27. Which is the tallest building in America?
    A.   the Empire State Building
    B.   the Space Needle
    C.   the Sears Tower
    D.   the Eiffel Tower

28. What world organization was founded so that leaders could meet to discuss world issues and to make treaties to keep the peace?
    A.   ACLU
    B.   NATO
    C.   UN
    D.   NCAA

29. The Wright Brothers are famous for
    A.   flying across the Atlantic in 1927.
    B.   the first successful airplane flight in history.
    C.   flying a hot-air balloon around the world in 80 days.
    D.   building the first jetliner.

Stay calm and focused. Don't let your mind wander.

30. What do historians study?
    A.   fossils and rocks
    B.   landforms
    C.   people and events of the past
    D.   the economy of regions

Name: _____ Date: _____

Lesson One: History and Culture (cont.)

Review

1. Social studies is about people, places, and events and when and how they happened.

2. Eliminate unreasonable answers first, and then make your choice.

3. Read maps, graphs, tables, and charts very carefully.

4. Stay calm and focused. Don't let your mind wander.

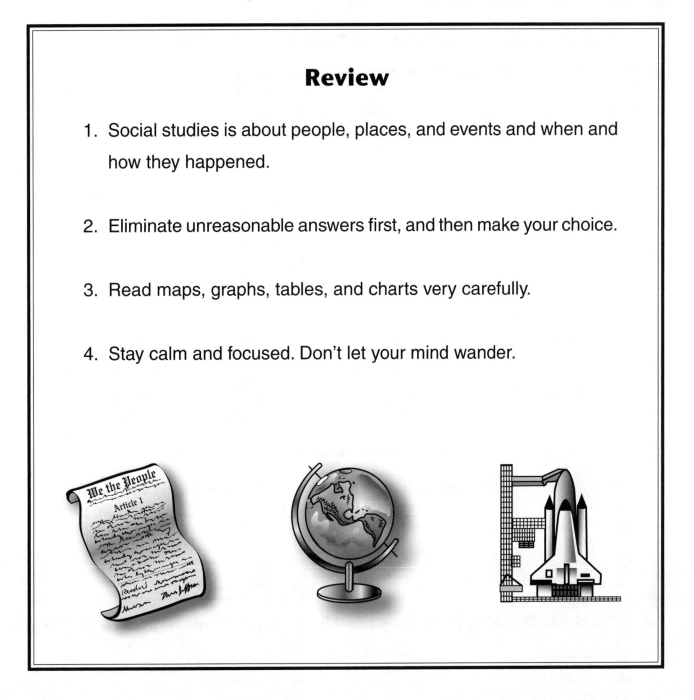

Name: _____ Date: _____

UNIT FIVE: SOCIAL STUDIES

Lesson Two: Civics, Government, and Economics

Directions: Choose the best answer for each question.

1. Producers make goods or provide services.
    Which of these is *not* a producer?
    A. author
    B. bus driver
    C. dentist
    D. shopper

Sharpen your brain by taking two deep, deep breaths.

2. What *goods* are sold by the producers in B?
    A. computers
    B. shoes
    C. pizzas
    D. automobiles

3. What *goods* are sold by the producers in D?
    A. computers
    B. shoes
    C. pizzas
    D. automobiles

4. What *goods* are sold by the producers in A?
    A. computers
    B. shoes
    C. pizzas
    D. automobiles

5. What *goods* are sold by the producers in C?
    A. computers
    B. shoes
    C. pizzas
    D. automobiles

Name: _____   Date: _____

Lesson Two: Civics, Government, and Economics (cont.)

6. All but one of these provide a *service*. Which does not?
   - A.   soccer player
   - B.   firefighter
   - C.   hairdresser
   - D.   teacher

7. Which one of these is a *consumer*?
   - A.   doctor
   - B.   shopper
   - C.   bookkeeper
   - D.   mail carrier

A.

B.

C.

8. Which drawing above shows too much supply, too little demand?
   - A.   A
   - B.   B
   - C.   C

9. Which drawing above shows too much demand, too little supply?
   - A.   A
   - B.   B
   - C.   C

Read and consider <u>all</u> answer choices; there may be a better choice farther down the list.

Name: _____ Date: _____

Lesson Two: Civics, Government, and Economics (cont.)

10. Which drawing on the previous page shows the supply equaling the demand?
    A.   A
    B.   B
    C.   C

11. Which of these is true?
    A.   The United States is a dictatorship with a government and laws made by the President.
    B.   The United States is a democracy with a government and laws based on the Constitution.
    C.   The United States is a monarchy with a government and laws made by the King.
    D.   The United States is a democracy with a government and laws made by the President.

12. Which one of these is true about the Bill of Rights?
    A.   The Bill of Rights guarantees rights for everyone born in the United States.
    B.   The Bill of Rights gives men of all races the right to vote.
    C.   The Bill of Rights abolishes slavery in the United States.
    D.   The Bill of Rights guarantees Americans certain rights that can't be taken away.

13. *"We the people of the United States, in Order to form a more perfect Union ..."* are the first words in what important document?
    A.   Declaration of Independence
    B.   United States Constitution
    C.   The Bill of Rights
    D.   The Articles of Confederation

14. Which of these is not a branch of the U.S. government?
    A.   legislative
    B.   executive
    C.   military
    D.   judicial

15. Which one of these is the responsibility of the **legislative** branch of the government?
    A.   to make the laws
    B.   to interpret the laws
    C.   to enforce the laws
    D.   to help the President do his job

Name: _____ Date: _____

Lesson Two: Civics, Government, and Economics (cont.)

16. What is a law?
   A.   a complaint brought to court
   B.   a rule that regulates the behavior of a group of people
   C.   the way in which a person behaves
   D.   a command or order

17. Congress has two parts, the House of Representatives and the
   A.   Department of Education.
   B.   Library of Congress.
   C.   Smithsonian Institute.
   D.   Senate.

18. Which one of these is the responsibility of the **executive** branch of the government?
   A.   to make the laws
   B.   to interpret the laws
   C.   to enforce the laws
   D.   to help Congress do its job

19. Who is the head of the executive branch of government?
   A.   the Speaker of the House of Representatives
   B.   the president
   C.   the Chief Justice of the Supreme Court
   D.   the Secretary of State

20. Which of these makes up the **judicial** branch of the government?
   A.   the president
   B.   the House of Representatives
   C.   the Supreme Court and lesser courts
   D.   the Congress

21. Which of these statements is true about our system of government?
   A.   The states share power with the national government.
   B.   The states do what the national government tells them to do.
   C.   The states do whatever they want, no matter what the national government tells them to do.
   D.   The states have more power than the national government.

22. Who is the head of the executive branch at the *state* level?
   A.   the president
   B.   the governor
   C.   the mayor
   D.   the principal

Name: _____ Date: _____

Lesson Two: Civics, Government, and Economics (cont.)

23. At which level of government does a mayor work?
   A. local
   B. regional
   C. state
   D. national

When you don't know the answer, take your best guess.

24. What is the minimum voting age in the United States?
   A. 18
   B. 20
   C. 21
   D. 16

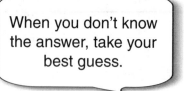

25. Who is the commander-in-chief of the United States military?
   A. the Attorney General
   B. the president
   C. the leader of Congress
   D. none of these

26. Which statement is *not* true?
   A. Most immigrants who come to the United States come from Asia and Latin America.
   B. Many immigrants who come to the United States have college degrees and professional experience.
   C. The majority of immigrants who come to the United States enter the U.S. illegally.
   D. Immigrants often come to the United States looking for better job opportunities.

27. Over 12 million immigrants entered the country through the immigration center in New York Harbor called
   A. Angel Island.
   B. Ellis Island.
   C. Boblo Island.
   D. Long Island.

28. Many immigrants, particularly Asian immigrants, entered the United States through this immigration center in California in the early twentieth century:
   A. Angel Island
   B. Ellis Island
   C. Boblo Island
   D. Long Island

Name: _____ Date: _____

Lesson Two: Civics, Government, and Economics (cont.)

29. To be eligible for United States citizenship, an immigrant must be:
    A.   18 years old or older.
    B.   a permanent legal resident of the United States.
    C.   able to read, write, and understand English.
    D.   all of the above.

30. All but which one of the following are the responsibilities of citizens?
    A.   arresting criminals
    B.   voting
    C.   obeying laws
    D.   respecting other people's rights and property

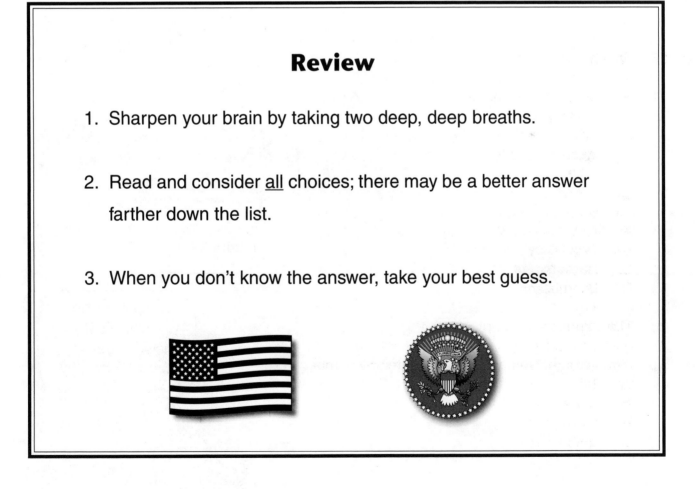

Review

1. Sharpen your brain by taking two deep, deep breaths.

2. Read and consider <u>all</u> choices; there may be a better answer farther down the list.

3. When you don't know the answer, take your best guess.

Name: _____ Date: _____

UNIT FIVE: SOCIAL STUDIES

Lesson Three: Geography

Directions: Use the landforms drawing in Figure 1 to answer questions 1–5.

1. Number 5 is an example of what type of landform?
   A. plain
   B. lake
   C. river
   D. swamp

2. What type of landform is represented in number 7?
   A. mountain
   B. hill
   C. volcano
   D. atoll

3. What type of landform is shown in number 3?
   A. atoll
   B. oasis
   C. lake
   D. island

4. What type of landform is represented by number 2?
   A. harbor
   B. isthmus
   C. cove
   D. strait

5. What type of landform is represented by number 11?
   A. bay
   B. ocean
   C. river
   D. lake

Figure 1

Social studies tests usually include questions about geography.

Name: _____ Date: _____

Lesson Three: Geography (cont.)

Directions: Study the drawing in Figure 2 carefully, and then answer questions 6–8.

6. Which landmark is the Eiffel Tower?
   A.   8
   B.   4
   C.   5
   D.   10

7. Which one of these landmarks was built to keep out invaders?
   A.   1
   B.   2
   C.   3
   D.   12

8. The ancient Romans held sporting events inside this circular arena.
   A.   2
   B.   12
   C.   11
   D.   10

Be sure you understand the kind of information the map, chart, or diagram is giving you.

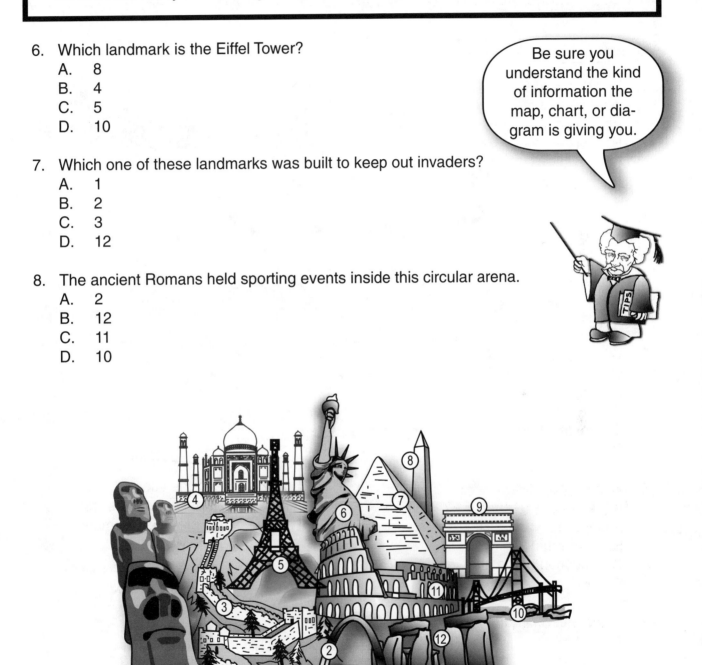

Figure 2

Name: _____ Date: _____

Lesson Three: Geography (cont.)

Directions: Study the map in Figure 3 to answer questions 9–11.

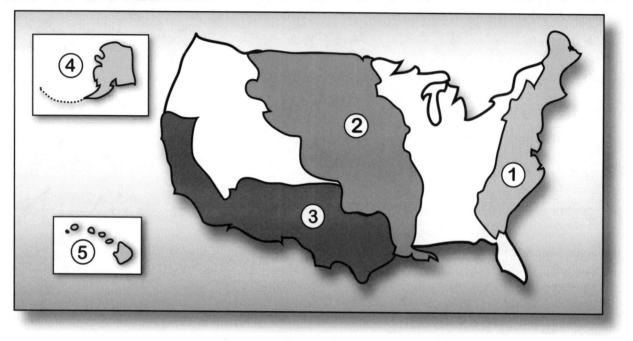

Figure 3

9. The original thirteen colonies are labeled _____ on this map.
   A. 1
   B. 2
   C. 3
   D. 4

10. What section of the map includes California?
   A. 1
   B. 2
   C. 3
   D. 5

11. What section of the map is the forty-ninth state?
   A. 4
   B. 3
   C. 2
   D. 5

Read the titles of maps, charts, and tables first. They provide information you need.

Name: _____ Date: _____

Lesson Three: Geography (cont.)

12. What is the capital of New York State?
    A. New York City
    B. Buffalo
    C. Albany
    D. None of these

13. Using a compass, which one of these is correct?
    A. NE is the opposite of SW.
    B. SE is the opposite of NE.
    C. NW is the opposite of SW.
    D. SW is the opposite of SE.

14. Which one of these cities is the farthest east?
    A. Detroit, Michigan
    B. Denver, Colorado
    C. Dover, New Jersey
    D. Des Moines, Iowa

15. Mexico, Canada, Bolivia, Costa Rica, and Honduras are all in which hemisphere?
    A. Northern
    B. Southern
    C. Eastern
    D. Western

16. The Mississippi River touches all but which one of these states?
    A. Minnesota
    B. Missouri
    C. Texas
    D. Illinois

Name: _____ Date: _____

Lesson Three: Geography (cont.)

Directions: Use the map in Figure 4 to find these bodies of water for questions 17–22.

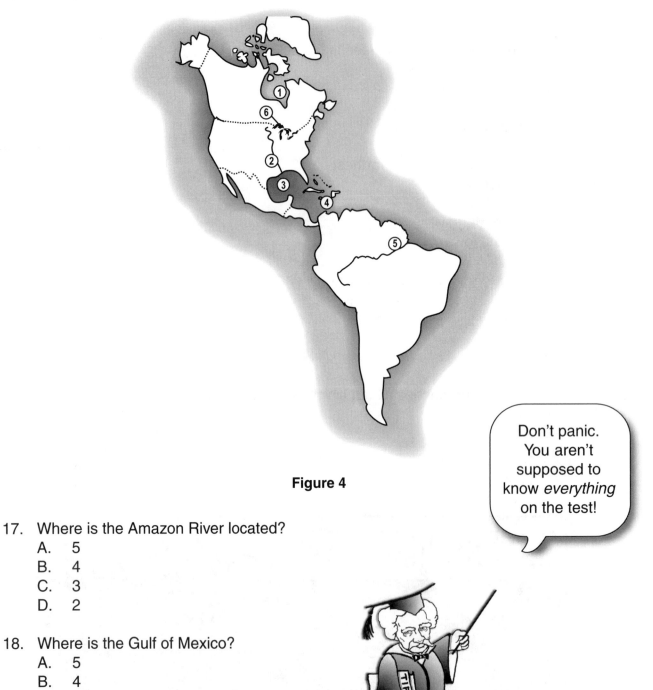

Figure 4

Don't panic. You aren't supposed to know *everything* on the test!

17. Where is the Amazon River located?
    A. 5
    B. 4
    C. 3
    D. 2

18. Where is the Gulf of Mexico?
    A. 5
    B. 4
    C. 3
    D. 2

Name: _____ Date: _____

Lesson Three: Geography (cont.)

19. Where is Lake Superior?
    A. 1
    B. 2
    C. 6
    D. 4

20. Where is the Hudson Bay?
    A. 1
    B. 2
    C. 6
    D. 4

21. Where is the Caribbean Sea?
    A. 2
    B. 3
    C. 4
    D. 1

22. Where is the Mississippi River?
    A. 6
    B. 2
    C. 3
    D. 4

Directions: Choose the correct answers for the following questions.

---

23. Which of these is not a country?
    A. Puerto Rico
    B. Africa
    C. Australia
    D. Cuba

24. All but which one of these would you expect to see on a resource map?
    A. natural gas
    B. forests
    C. climate
    D. coal

25. All of these are located in the Midwest except:
    A. the Missouri River.
    B. the Rio Grande.
    C. the Mississippi River.
    D. Lake Michigan.

Name: _____ Date: _____

Lesson Three: Geography (cont.)

Directions: Read the chart in Figure 5 carefully, and then answer questions 26–27.

NATIVE AMERICAN POPULATION PER STATE

❶	California	333,346	❾	New York	82,461
❷	Oklahoma	273,230	❿	South Dakota	62,283
❸	Arizona	255,879	⓫	Michigan	58,479
❹	New Mexico	173,483	⓬	Montana	56,068
❺	Texas	118,362	⓭	Minnesota	54,967
❻	North Carolina	99,551	⓮	Florida	53,541
❼	Alaska	98,043	⓯	Wisconsin	47,228
❽	Washington	93,301	⓰	Oregon	45,211

Figure 5

26. Which state has the largest Native American population?
    A. California
    B. Oklahoma
    C. Arizona
    D. New Mexico

27. Which state has the smallest Native American population?
    A. Minnesota
    B. Florida
    C. New York
    D. Oregon

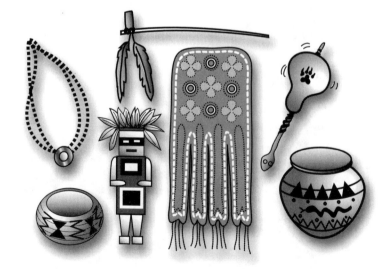

Name: _____ Date: _____

Lesson Three: Geography (cont.)

Directions: Use the information in Figure 6 to answer questions 28–30.

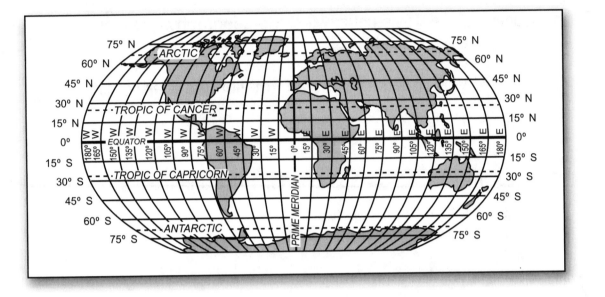

Figure 6

28. Which continent touches both the Prime Meridian and the equator?
    A. South America
    B. North America
    C. Australia
    D. Africa

29. How would you describe the Prime Meridian in degrees?
    A. 0° longitude
    B. 0° latitude
    C. 140°S latitude
    D. 120°W longitude

30. Which of these cities would be closest to 38°N and 77°W?
    A. Rome, Italy
    B. Sydney, Australia
    C. Athens, Greece
    D. Washington, D.C., USA

Name: _____ Date: _____

Lesson Three: Geography (cont.)

Review

1. Social studies tests usually include geography questions.

2. Be sure you understand the information the map, chart, or diagram is giving you.

3. Read the title of the maps, charts, and diagrams first. They provide the information you need.

4. Don't panic. You aren't supposed to know *everything* on the test!

Name: _____ Date: _____

Standardized Testing Grade 4 Answer Sheet

School:	Student Name			
Teacher:	Last		First	MI

Female ◯ **Male** ◯

Birth Date

Month	Day	Year
Jan ◯	⓪ ⓪	⓪ ⓪
Feb ◯	① ①	① ①
Mar ◯	② ②	② ②
Apr ◯	③ ③	③ ③
May ◯	④	④ ④
Jun ◯	⑤	⑤ ⑤
Jul ◯	⑥	⑥ ⑥
Aug ◯	⑦	⑦ ⑦
Sep ◯	⑧	⑧ ⑧
Oct ◯	⑨	⑨ ⑨
Nov ◯		
Dec ◯		

Grade ③ ④ ⑤ ⑥ ⑦ ⑧

(Student name grid with bubbles A–Z for each letter column)

Unit One: Reading   Lesson One: Vocabulary

1. Ⓐ Ⓑ Ⓒ Ⓓ	7. Ⓐ Ⓑ Ⓒ Ⓓ	13. Ⓐ Ⓑ Ⓒ Ⓓ	19. Ⓐ Ⓑ Ⓒ Ⓓ	25. Ⓐ Ⓑ Ⓒ Ⓓ
2. Ⓐ Ⓑ Ⓒ Ⓓ	8. Ⓐ Ⓑ Ⓒ Ⓓ	14. Ⓐ Ⓑ Ⓒ Ⓓ	20. Ⓐ Ⓑ Ⓒ Ⓓ	26. Ⓐ Ⓑ Ⓒ Ⓓ
3. Ⓐ Ⓑ Ⓒ Ⓓ	9. Ⓐ Ⓑ Ⓒ Ⓓ	15. Ⓐ Ⓑ Ⓒ Ⓓ	21. Ⓐ Ⓑ Ⓒ Ⓓ	27. Ⓐ Ⓑ Ⓒ Ⓓ
4. Ⓐ Ⓑ Ⓒ Ⓓ	10. Ⓐ Ⓑ Ⓒ Ⓓ	16. Ⓐ Ⓑ Ⓒ Ⓓ	22. Ⓐ Ⓑ Ⓒ Ⓓ	28. Ⓐ Ⓑ Ⓒ Ⓓ
5. Ⓐ Ⓑ Ⓒ Ⓓ	11. Ⓐ Ⓑ Ⓒ Ⓓ	17. Ⓐ Ⓑ Ⓒ Ⓓ	23. Ⓐ Ⓑ Ⓒ Ⓓ	29. Ⓐ Ⓑ Ⓒ Ⓓ
6. Ⓐ Ⓑ Ⓒ Ⓓ	12. Ⓐ Ⓑ Ⓒ Ⓓ	18. Ⓐ Ⓑ Ⓒ Ⓓ	24. Ⓐ Ⓑ Ⓒ Ⓓ	30. Ⓐ Ⓑ Ⓒ Ⓓ

Name: _____ Date: _____

Standardized Testing Grade 4 Answer Sheet

Unit One: Reading   Lesson Two: Word Analysis

1. (A) (B) (C) (D)   6. (A) (B) (C) (D)   11. (A) (B) (C) (D)   16. (A) (B) (C) (D)   21. (A) (B) (C) (D)
2. (A) (B) (C) (D)   7. (A) (B) (C) (D)   12. (A) (B) (C) (D)   17. (A) (B) (C) (D)   22. (A) (B) (C) (D)
3. (A) (B) (C) (D)   8. (A) (B) (C) (D)   13. (A) (B) (C) (D)   18. (A) (B) (C) (D)   23. (A) (B) (C) (D)
4. (A) (B) (C) (D)   9. (A) (B) (C) (D)   14. (A) (B) (C) (D)   19. (A) (B) (C) (D)   24. (A) (B) (C) (D)
5. (A) (B) (C) (D)   10. (A) (B) (C) (D)   15. (A) (B) (C) (D)   20. (A) (B) (C) (D)   25. (A) (B) (C) (D)

Unit One: Reading   Lesson Three: Comprehension

1. (A) (B) (C) (D)   7. (A) (B) (C) (D)   13. (A) (B) (C) (D)   19. (A) (B) (C) (D)   25. (A) (B) (C) (D)
2. (A) (B) (C) (D)   8. (A) (B) (C) (D)   14. (A) (B) (C) (D)   20. (A) (B) (C) (D)   26. (A) (B) (C) (D)
3. (A) (B) (C) (D)   9. (A) (B) (C) (D)   15. (A) (B) (C) (D)   21. (A) (B) (C) (D)   27. (A) (B) (C) (D)
4. (A) (B) (C) (D)   10. (A) (B) (C) (D)   16. (A) (B) (C) (D)   22. (A) (B) (C) (D)   28. (A) (B) (C) (D)
5. (A) (B) (C) (D)   11. (A) (B) (C) (D)   17. (A) (B) (C) (D)   23. (A) (B) (C) (D)   29. (A) (B) (C) (D)
6. (A) (B) (C) (D)   12. (A) (B) (C) (D)   18. (A) (B) (C) (D)   24. (A) (B) (C) (D)   30. (A) (B) (C) (D)

Unit Two: Language   Lesson One: Mechanics

1. (A) (B) (C) (D)   10. (A) (B) (C) (D)   19. (A) (B) (C) (D)   28. (A) (B) (C) (D)   37. (A) (B) (C) (D)
2. (A) (B) (C) (D)   11. (A) (B) (C) (D)   20. (A) (B) (C) (D)   29. (A) (B) (C) (D)   38. (A) (B) (C) (D)
3. (A) (B) (C) (D)   12. (A) (B) (C) (D)   21. (A) (B) (C) (D)   30. (A) (B) (C) (D)   39. (A) (B) (C) (D)
4. (A) (B) (C) (D)   13. (A) (B) (C) (D)   22. (A) (B) (C) (D)   31. (A) (B) (C) (D)   40. (A) (B) (C) (D)
5. (A) (B) (C) (D)   14. (A) (B) (C) (D)   23. (A) (B) (C) (D)   32. (A) (B) (C) (D)   41. (A) (B) (C) (D)
6. (A) (B) (C) (D)   15. (A) (B) (C) (D)   24. (A) (B) (C) (D)   33. (A) (B) (C) (D)   42. (A) (B) (C) (D)
7. (A) (B) (C) (D)   16. (A) (B) (C) (D)   25. (A) (B) (C) (D)   34. (A) (B) (C) (D)   43. (A) (B) (C) (D)
8. (A) (B) (C) (D)   17. (A) (B) (C) (D)   26. (A) (B) (C) (D)   35. (A) (B) (C) (D)   44. (A) (B) (C) (D)
9. (A) (B) (C) (D)   18. (A) (B) (C) (D)   27. (A) (B) (C) (D)   36. (A) (B) (C) (D)   45. (A) (B) (C) (D)

Name: _____   Date: _____

Standardized Testing Grade 4 Answer Sheet

Unit Two: Language   Lesson Two: Expression

1. (A) (B) (C) (D)   10. (A) (B) (C) (D)   19. (A) (B) (C) (D)   28. (A) (B) (C) (D)   37. (A) (B) (C) (D)
2. (A) (B) (C) (D)   11. (A) (B) (C) (D)   20. (A) (B) (C) (D)   29. (A) (B) (C) (D)   38. (A) (B) (C) (D)
3. (A) (B) (C) (D)   12. (A) (B) (C) (D)   21. (A) (B) (C) (D)   30. (A) (B) (C) (D)   39. (A) (B) (C) (D)
4. (A) (B) (C) (D)   13. (A) (B) (C) (D)   22. (A) (B) (C) (D)   31. (A) (B) (C) (D)   40. (A) (B) (C) (D)
5. (A) (B) (C) (D)   14. (A) (B) (C) (D)   23. (A) (B) (C) (D)   32. (A) (B) (C) (D)   41. (A) (B) (C) (D)
6. (A) (B) (C) (D)   15. (A) (B) (C) (D)   24. (A) (B) (C) (D)   33. (A) (B) (C) (D)   42. (A) (B) (C) (D)
7. (A) (B) (C) (D)   16. (A) (B) (C) (D)   25. (A) (B) (C) (D)   34. (A) (B) (C) (D)   43. (A) (B) (C) (D)
8. (A) (B) (C) (D)   17. (A) (B) (C) (D)   26. (A) (B) (C) (D)   35. (A) (B) (C) (D)   44. (A) (B) (C) (D)
9. (A) (B) (C) (D)   18. (A) (B) (C) (D)   27. (A) (B) (C) (D)   36. (A) (B) (C) (D)   45. (A) (B) (C) (D)

Unit Two: Language   Lesson Three: Information Skills

1. (A) (B) (C) (D)   9. (A) (B) (C) (D)   17. (A) (B) (C) (D)   25. (A) (B) (C) (D)   33. (A) (B) (C) (D)
2. (A) (B) (C) (D)   10. (A) (B) (C) (D)   18. (A) (B) (C) (D)   26. (A) (B) (C) (D)   34. (A) (B) (C) (D)
3. (A) (B) (C) (D)   11. (A) (B) (C) (D)   19. (A) (B) (C) (D)   27. (A) (B) (C) (D)   35. (A) (B) (C) (D)
4. (A) (B) (C) (D)   12. (A) (B) (C) (D)   20. (A) (B) (C) (D)   28. (A) (B) (C) (D)   36. (A) (B) (C) (D)
5. (A) (B) (C) (D)   13. (A) (B) (C) (D)   21. (A) (B) (C) (D)   29. (A) (B) (C) (D)   37. (A) (B) (C) (D)
6. (A) (B) (C) (D)   14. (A) (B) (C) (D)   22. (A) (B) (C) (D)   30. (A) (B) (C) (D)   38. (A) (B) (C) (D)
7. (A) (B) (C) (D)   15. (A) (B) (C) (D)   23. (A) (B) (C) (D)   31. (A) (B) (C) (D)   39. (A) (B) (C) (D)
8. (A) (B) (C) (D)   16. (A) (B) (C) (D)   24. (A) (B) (C) (D)   32. (A) (B) (C) (D)   40. (A) (B) (C) (D)

Unit Three: Mathematics   Lesson One: Concepts

1. (A) (B) (C) (D)   7. (A) (B) (C) (D)   13. (A) (B) (C) (D)   19. (A) (B) (C) (D)   25. (A) (B) (C) (D)
2. (A) (B) (C) (D)   8. (A) (B) (C) (D)   14. (A) (B) (C) (D)   20. (A) (B) (C) (D)   26. (A) (B) (C) (D)
3. (A) (B) (C) (D)   9. (A) (B) (C) (D)   15. (A) (B) (C) (D)   21. (A) (B) (C) (D)   27. (A) (B) (C) (D)
4. (A) (B) (C) (D)   10. (A) (B) (C) (D)   16. (A) (B) (C) (D)   22. (A) (B) (C) (D)   28. (A) (B) (C) (D)
5. (A) (B) (C) (D)   11. (A) (B) (C) (D)   17. (A) (B) (C) (D)   23. (A) (B) (C) (D)   29. (A) (B) (C) (D)
6. (A) (B) (C) (D)   12. (A) (B) (C) (D)   18. (A) (B) (C) (D)   24. (A) (B) (C) (D)   30. (A) (B) (C) (D)

Name: _____   Date: _____

Standardized Testing Grade 4 Answer Sheet

Unit Three: Mathematics   Lesson Two: Computation

1. Ⓐ Ⓑ Ⓒ Ⓓ	8. Ⓐ Ⓑ Ⓒ Ⓓ	15. Ⓐ Ⓑ Ⓒ Ⓓ	22. Ⓐ Ⓑ Ⓒ Ⓓ	29. Ⓐ Ⓑ Ⓒ Ⓓ
2. Ⓐ Ⓑ Ⓒ Ⓓ	9. Ⓐ Ⓑ Ⓒ Ⓓ	16. Ⓐ Ⓑ Ⓒ Ⓓ	23. Ⓐ Ⓑ Ⓒ Ⓓ	30. Ⓐ Ⓑ Ⓒ Ⓓ
3. Ⓐ Ⓑ Ⓒ Ⓓ	10. Ⓐ Ⓑ Ⓒ Ⓓ	17. Ⓐ Ⓑ Ⓒ Ⓓ	24. Ⓐ Ⓑ Ⓒ Ⓓ	31. Ⓐ Ⓑ Ⓒ Ⓓ
4. Ⓐ Ⓑ Ⓒ Ⓓ	11. Ⓐ Ⓑ Ⓒ Ⓓ	18. Ⓐ Ⓑ Ⓒ Ⓓ	25. Ⓐ Ⓑ Ⓒ Ⓓ	32. Ⓐ Ⓑ Ⓒ Ⓓ
5. Ⓐ Ⓑ Ⓒ Ⓓ	12. Ⓐ Ⓑ Ⓒ Ⓓ	19. Ⓐ Ⓑ Ⓒ Ⓓ	26. Ⓐ Ⓑ Ⓒ Ⓓ	33. Ⓐ Ⓑ Ⓒ Ⓓ
6. Ⓐ Ⓑ Ⓒ Ⓓ	13. Ⓐ Ⓑ Ⓒ Ⓓ	20. Ⓐ Ⓑ Ⓒ Ⓓ	27. Ⓐ Ⓑ Ⓒ Ⓓ	34. Ⓐ Ⓑ Ⓒ Ⓓ
7. Ⓐ Ⓑ Ⓒ Ⓓ	14. Ⓐ Ⓑ Ⓒ Ⓓ	21. Ⓐ Ⓑ Ⓒ Ⓓ	28. Ⓐ Ⓑ Ⓒ Ⓓ	35. Ⓐ Ⓑ Ⓒ Ⓓ

Unit Three: Mathematics   Lesson Three: Problem Solving and Reasoning

1. Ⓐ Ⓑ Ⓒ Ⓓ	6. Ⓐ Ⓑ Ⓒ Ⓓ	11. Ⓐ Ⓑ Ⓒ Ⓓ	16. Ⓐ Ⓑ Ⓒ Ⓓ	21. Ⓐ Ⓑ Ⓒ Ⓓ
2. Ⓐ Ⓑ Ⓒ Ⓓ	7. Ⓐ Ⓑ Ⓒ Ⓓ	12. Ⓐ Ⓑ Ⓒ Ⓓ	17. Ⓐ Ⓑ Ⓒ Ⓓ	22. Ⓐ Ⓑ Ⓒ Ⓓ
3. Ⓐ Ⓑ Ⓒ Ⓓ	8. Ⓐ Ⓑ Ⓒ Ⓓ	13. Ⓐ Ⓑ Ⓒ Ⓓ	18. Ⓐ Ⓑ Ⓒ Ⓓ	23. Ⓐ Ⓑ Ⓒ Ⓓ
4. Ⓐ Ⓑ Ⓒ Ⓓ	9. Ⓐ Ⓑ Ⓒ Ⓓ	14. Ⓐ Ⓑ Ⓒ Ⓓ	19. Ⓐ Ⓑ Ⓒ Ⓓ	24. Ⓐ Ⓑ Ⓒ Ⓓ
5. Ⓐ Ⓑ Ⓒ Ⓓ	10. Ⓐ Ⓑ Ⓒ Ⓓ	15. Ⓐ Ⓑ Ⓒ Ⓓ	20. Ⓐ Ⓑ Ⓒ Ⓓ	25. Ⓐ Ⓑ Ⓒ Ⓓ

Unit Four: Science   Lesson One: Process and Inquiry

1. Ⓐ Ⓑ Ⓒ Ⓓ	6. Ⓐ Ⓑ Ⓒ Ⓓ	11. Ⓐ Ⓑ Ⓒ Ⓓ	16. Ⓐ Ⓑ Ⓒ Ⓓ	21. Ⓐ Ⓑ Ⓒ Ⓓ
2. Ⓐ Ⓑ Ⓒ Ⓓ	7. Ⓐ Ⓑ Ⓒ Ⓓ	12. Ⓐ Ⓑ Ⓒ Ⓓ	17. Ⓐ Ⓑ Ⓒ Ⓓ	22. Ⓐ Ⓑ Ⓒ Ⓓ
3. Ⓐ Ⓑ Ⓒ Ⓓ	8. Ⓐ Ⓑ Ⓒ Ⓓ	13. Ⓐ Ⓑ Ⓒ Ⓓ	18. Ⓐ Ⓑ Ⓒ Ⓓ	23. Ⓐ Ⓑ Ⓒ Ⓓ
4. Ⓐ Ⓑ Ⓒ Ⓓ	9. Ⓐ Ⓑ Ⓒ Ⓓ	14. Ⓐ Ⓑ Ⓒ Ⓓ	19. Ⓐ Ⓑ Ⓒ Ⓓ	24. Ⓐ Ⓑ Ⓒ Ⓓ
5. Ⓐ Ⓑ Ⓒ Ⓓ	10. Ⓐ Ⓑ Ⓒ Ⓓ	15. Ⓐ Ⓑ Ⓒ Ⓓ	20. Ⓐ Ⓑ Ⓒ Ⓓ	25. Ⓐ Ⓑ Ⓒ Ⓓ

Name: _____ Date: _____

Standardized Testing Grade 4 Answer Sheet

Unit Four: Science   **Lesson Two: Concepts**

1. Ⓐ Ⓑ Ⓒ Ⓓ	9. Ⓐ Ⓑ Ⓒ Ⓓ	17. Ⓐ Ⓑ Ⓒ Ⓓ	25. Ⓐ Ⓑ Ⓒ Ⓓ	33. Ⓐ Ⓑ Ⓒ Ⓓ
2. Ⓐ Ⓑ Ⓒ Ⓓ	10. Ⓐ Ⓑ Ⓒ Ⓓ	18. Ⓐ Ⓑ Ⓒ Ⓓ	26. Ⓐ Ⓑ Ⓒ Ⓓ	34. Ⓐ Ⓑ Ⓒ Ⓓ
3. Ⓐ Ⓑ Ⓒ Ⓓ	11. Ⓐ Ⓑ Ⓒ Ⓓ	19. Ⓐ Ⓑ Ⓒ Ⓓ	27. Ⓐ Ⓑ Ⓒ Ⓓ	35. Ⓐ Ⓑ Ⓒ Ⓓ
4. Ⓐ Ⓑ Ⓒ Ⓓ	12. Ⓐ Ⓑ Ⓒ Ⓓ	20. Ⓐ Ⓑ Ⓒ Ⓓ	28. Ⓐ Ⓑ Ⓒ Ⓓ	36. Ⓐ Ⓑ Ⓒ Ⓓ
5. Ⓐ Ⓑ Ⓒ Ⓓ	13. Ⓐ Ⓑ Ⓒ Ⓓ	21. Ⓐ Ⓑ Ⓒ Ⓓ	29. Ⓐ Ⓑ Ⓒ Ⓓ	37. Ⓐ Ⓑ Ⓒ Ⓓ
6. Ⓐ Ⓑ Ⓒ Ⓓ	14. Ⓐ Ⓑ Ⓒ Ⓓ	22. Ⓐ Ⓑ Ⓒ Ⓓ	30. Ⓐ Ⓑ Ⓒ Ⓓ	38. Ⓐ Ⓑ Ⓒ Ⓓ
7. Ⓐ Ⓑ Ⓒ Ⓓ	15. Ⓐ Ⓑ Ⓒ Ⓓ	23. Ⓐ Ⓑ Ⓒ Ⓓ	31. Ⓐ Ⓑ Ⓒ Ⓓ	39. Ⓐ Ⓑ Ⓒ Ⓓ
8. Ⓐ Ⓑ Ⓒ Ⓓ	16. Ⓐ Ⓑ Ⓒ Ⓓ	24. Ⓐ Ⓑ Ⓒ Ⓓ	32. Ⓐ Ⓑ Ⓒ Ⓓ	40. Ⓐ Ⓑ Ⓒ Ⓓ

Unit Five: Social Studies   **Lesson One: History and Culture**

1. Ⓐ Ⓑ Ⓒ Ⓓ	7. Ⓐ Ⓑ Ⓒ Ⓓ	13. Ⓐ Ⓑ Ⓒ Ⓓ	19. Ⓐ Ⓑ Ⓒ Ⓓ	25. Ⓐ Ⓑ Ⓒ Ⓓ
2. Ⓐ Ⓑ Ⓒ Ⓓ	8. Ⓐ Ⓑ Ⓒ Ⓓ	14. Ⓐ Ⓑ Ⓒ Ⓓ	20. Ⓐ Ⓑ Ⓒ Ⓓ	26. Ⓐ Ⓑ Ⓒ Ⓓ
3. Ⓐ Ⓑ Ⓒ Ⓓ	9. Ⓐ Ⓑ Ⓒ Ⓓ	15. Ⓐ Ⓑ Ⓒ Ⓓ	21. Ⓐ Ⓑ Ⓒ Ⓓ	27. Ⓐ Ⓑ Ⓒ Ⓓ
4. Ⓐ Ⓑ Ⓒ Ⓓ	10. Ⓐ Ⓑ Ⓒ Ⓓ	16. Ⓐ Ⓑ Ⓒ Ⓓ	22. Ⓐ Ⓑ Ⓒ Ⓓ	28. Ⓐ Ⓑ Ⓒ Ⓓ
5. Ⓐ Ⓑ Ⓒ Ⓓ	11. Ⓐ Ⓑ Ⓒ Ⓓ	17. Ⓐ Ⓑ Ⓒ Ⓓ	23. Ⓐ Ⓑ Ⓒ Ⓓ	29. Ⓐ Ⓑ Ⓒ Ⓓ
6. Ⓐ Ⓑ Ⓒ Ⓓ	12. Ⓐ Ⓑ Ⓒ Ⓓ	18. Ⓐ Ⓑ Ⓒ Ⓓ	24. Ⓐ Ⓑ Ⓒ Ⓓ	30. Ⓐ Ⓑ Ⓒ Ⓓ

Unit Five: Social Studies   **Lesson Two: Civics, Government, and Economics**

1. Ⓐ Ⓑ Ⓒ Ⓓ	7. Ⓐ Ⓑ Ⓒ Ⓓ	13. Ⓐ Ⓑ Ⓒ Ⓓ	19. Ⓐ Ⓑ Ⓒ Ⓓ	25. Ⓐ Ⓑ Ⓒ Ⓓ
2. Ⓐ Ⓑ Ⓒ Ⓓ	8. Ⓐ Ⓑ Ⓒ Ⓓ	14. Ⓐ Ⓑ Ⓒ Ⓓ	20. Ⓐ Ⓑ Ⓒ Ⓓ	26. Ⓐ Ⓑ Ⓒ Ⓓ
3. Ⓐ Ⓑ Ⓒ Ⓓ	9. Ⓐ Ⓑ Ⓒ Ⓓ	15. Ⓐ Ⓑ Ⓒ Ⓓ	21. Ⓐ Ⓑ Ⓒ Ⓓ	27. Ⓐ Ⓑ Ⓒ Ⓓ
4. Ⓐ Ⓑ Ⓒ Ⓓ	10. Ⓐ Ⓑ Ⓒ Ⓓ	16. Ⓐ Ⓑ Ⓒ Ⓓ	22. Ⓐ Ⓑ Ⓒ Ⓓ	28. Ⓐ Ⓑ Ⓒ Ⓓ
5. Ⓐ Ⓑ Ⓒ Ⓓ	11. Ⓐ Ⓑ Ⓒ Ⓓ	17. Ⓐ Ⓑ Ⓒ Ⓓ	23. Ⓐ Ⓑ Ⓒ Ⓓ	29. Ⓐ Ⓑ Ⓒ Ⓓ
6. Ⓐ Ⓑ Ⓒ Ⓓ	12. Ⓐ Ⓑ Ⓒ Ⓓ	18. Ⓐ Ⓑ Ⓒ Ⓓ	24. Ⓐ Ⓑ Ⓒ Ⓓ	30. Ⓐ Ⓑ Ⓒ Ⓓ

Name: _____ Date: _____

Standardized Testing Grade 4 Answer Sheet

Unit Five: Social Studies   **Lesson Three: Geography**

1. Ⓐ Ⓑ Ⓒ Ⓓ   7. Ⓐ Ⓑ Ⓒ Ⓓ   13. Ⓐ Ⓑ Ⓒ Ⓓ   19. Ⓐ Ⓑ Ⓒ Ⓓ   25. Ⓐ Ⓑ Ⓒ Ⓓ
2. Ⓐ Ⓑ Ⓒ Ⓓ   8. Ⓐ Ⓑ Ⓒ Ⓓ   14. Ⓐ Ⓑ Ⓒ Ⓓ   20. Ⓐ Ⓑ Ⓒ Ⓓ   26. Ⓐ Ⓑ Ⓒ Ⓓ
3. Ⓐ Ⓑ Ⓒ Ⓓ   9. Ⓐ Ⓑ Ⓒ Ⓓ   15. Ⓐ Ⓑ Ⓒ Ⓓ   21. Ⓐ Ⓑ Ⓒ Ⓓ   27. Ⓐ Ⓑ Ⓒ Ⓓ
4. Ⓐ Ⓑ Ⓒ Ⓓ   10. Ⓐ Ⓑ Ⓒ Ⓓ   16. Ⓐ Ⓑ Ⓒ Ⓓ   22. Ⓐ Ⓑ Ⓒ Ⓓ   28. Ⓐ Ⓑ Ⓒ Ⓓ
5. Ⓐ Ⓑ Ⓒ Ⓓ   11. Ⓐ Ⓑ Ⓒ Ⓓ   17. Ⓐ Ⓑ Ⓒ Ⓓ   23. Ⓐ Ⓑ Ⓒ Ⓓ   29. Ⓐ Ⓑ Ⓒ Ⓓ
6. Ⓐ Ⓑ Ⓒ Ⓓ   12. Ⓐ Ⓑ Ⓒ Ⓓ   18. Ⓐ Ⓑ Ⓒ Ⓓ   24. Ⓐ Ⓑ Ⓒ Ⓓ   30. Ⓐ Ⓑ Ⓒ Ⓓ

Standardized Testing Grade 4 Answer Key

Unit One: Reading **Lesson One: Vocabulary**

1. A B **C** D	7. **A** B C D	13. **A** B C D	19. **A** B C D	25. A **B** C D
2. A **B** C D	8. A B C **D**	14. A B **C** D	20. A **B** C D	26. A B C **D**
3. **A** B C D	9. **A** B C D	15. A B C **D**	21. A **B** C D	27. A **B** C D
4. A B C **D**	10. A B C **D**	16. **A** B C D	22. A B C **D**	28. A B **C** D
5. A B C **D**	11. A **B** C D	17. A B **C** D	23. **A** B C D	29. **A** B C D
6. A **B** C D	12. A B **C** D	18. A B C **D**	24. A B **C** D	30. A B **C** D

Standardized Testing Grade 4 Answer Key

Unit One: Reading   Lesson Two: Word Analysis

1. **A** B C D	6. A B **C** D	11. A B C **D**	16. A **B** C D	21. A B C **D**
2. A **B** C D	7. A **B** C D	12. **A** B C D	17. A B C **D**	22. **A** B C D
3. **A** B C D	8. **A** B C D	13. A **B** C D	18. **A** B C D	23. A **B** C D
4. A B C **D**	9. A **B** C D	14. A B **C** D	19. A B **C** D	24. A B **C** D
5. A B **C** D	10. A B C **D**	15. A B C **D**	20. A **B** C D	25. A B **C** D

Unit One: Reading   Lesson Three: Comprehension

1. A B **C** D	7. A B **C** D	13. **A** B C D	19. A **B** C D	25. A **B** C D
2. A **B** C D	8. A **B** C D	14. A **B** C D	20. A B **C** D	26. A B C **D**
3. A B C **D**	9. A B **C** D	15. A B C **D**	21. A **B** C D	27. **A** B C D
4. A B **C** D	10. A **B** C D	16. A B **C** D	22. **A** B C D	28. A **B** C D
5. **A** B C D	11. A B **C** D	17. A **B** C D	23. A B **C** D	29. A B C **D**
6. **A** B C D	12. **A** B C D	18. **A** B C D	24. **A** B C D	30. A **B** C D

Unit Two: Language   Lesson One: Mechanics

1. A B **C** D	10. **A** B C D	19. A **B** C D	28. A **B** C D	37. **A** B C D
2. **A** B C D	11. A B **C** D	20. **A** B C D	29. A B **C** D	38. A **B** C D
3. A B C **D**	12. A **B** C D	21. A B C **D**	30. A B C **D**	39. **A** B C D
4. A **B** C D	13. A B C **D**	22. **A** B C D	31. A B **C** D	40. A B C **D**
5. A **B** C D	14. **A** B C D	23. A **B** C D	32. **A** B C D	41. A B **C** D
6. A B **C** D	15. A **B** C D	24. A B **C** D	33. A **B** C D	42. A B C **D**
7. A B **C** D	16. A B **C** D	25. **A** B C D	34. A B **C** D	43. **A** B C D
8. A **B** C D	17. **A** B C D	26. **A** B C D	35. A B **C** D	44. A **B** C D
9. A B **C** D	18. A B **C** D	27. A **B** C D	36. A **B** C D	45. A **B** C D

Standardized Testing Grade 4 Answer Key

Unit Two: Language   Lesson Two: Expression

1. B	10. B	19. B	28. B	37. D
2. A	11. C	20. D	29. A	38. C
3. C	12. B	21. A	30. D	39. B
4. C	13. B	22. B	31. B	40. A
5. A	14. C	23. A	32. A	41. C
6. C	15. A	24. C	33. C	42. D
7. B	16. B	25. D	34. D	43. D
8. A	17. C	26. A	35. A	44. B
9. C	18. A	27. C	36. A	45. A

Unit Two: Language   Lesson Three: Information Skills

1. C	9. D	17. B	25. C	33. B
2. A	10. C	18. C	26. B	34. A
3. D	11. B	19. A	27. A	35. A
4. B	12. D	20. C	28. C	36. C
5. C	13. D	21. D	29. A	37. A
6. A	14. D	22. B	30. C	38. D
7. B	15. A	23. A	31. A	39. A
8. A	16. C	24. B	32. D	40. B

Unit Three: Mathematics   Lesson One: Concepts

1. C	7. A	13. C	19. A	25. A
2. B	8. B	14. B	20. C	26. C
3. C	9. B	15. C	21. B	27. C
4. B	10. B	16. B	22. A	28. B
5. D	11. C	17. C	23. C	29. A
6. B	12. B	18. A	24. D	30. B

Standardized Testing Grade 4 Answer Key

Unit Three: Mathematics   Lesson Two: Computation

1. B	8. A	15. B	22. B	29. D
2. C	9. C	16. C	23. D	30. A
3. D	10. B	17. B	24. A	31. C
4. D	11. C	18. C	25. D	32. B
5. B	12. A	19. A	26. C	33. C
6. A	13. D	20. A	27. D	34. A
7. B	14. B	21. C	28. C	35. D

Unit Three: Mathematics   Lesson Three: Problem Solving and Reasoning

1. A	6. C	11. C	16. A	21. B
2. B	7. C	12. B	17. D	22. A
3. C	8. C	13. B	18. B	23. C
4. A	9. C	14. C	19. C	24. B
5. D	10. B	15. D	20. A	25. C

Unit Four: Science   Lesson One: Process and Inquiry

1. D	6. A	11. B	16. C	21. C
2. B	7. D	12. C	17. B	22. B
3. C	8. A	13. D	18. B	23. A
4. D	9. C	14. C	19. B	24. C
5. B	10. C	15. D	20. B	25. C